Emanuel Green

The march of William of Orange through Somerset

with a notice of other local events in the time of King James II, A.D. 1688

Emanuel Green

The march of William of Orange through Somerset
with a notice of other local events in the time of King James II, A.D. 1688

ISBN/EAN: 9783744744904

Printed in Europe, USA, Canada, Australia, Japan

Cover: Foto ©ninafisch / pixelio.de

More available books at **www.hansebooks.com**

Emanuel Green

The march of William of Orange through Somerset
with a notice of other local events in the time of King James II, A.D. 1688

ISBN/EAN: 9783744744904

Printed in Europe, USA, Canada, Australia, Japan

Cover: Foto ©ninafisch / pixelio.de

More available books at **www.hansebooks.com**

THE MARCH

OF

William of Orange

THROUGH

Somerset

WITH A NOTICE OF OTHER LOCAL EVENTS IN THE TIME OF

King James II.

A.D. 1688

BY

EMANUEL GREEN, F.S.A.

MEMBER OF THE SOMERSET ARCHÆOLOGICAL AND NATURAL HISTORY SOCIETY
ETC.

London

PRINTED FOR THE AUTHOR

1892

PREFACE

On finding in the Bodleian Library the manuscripts herein used, they were at first extracted as suitable for a 'paper.' Then, as some introduction seemed advisable, other search was made for more material; but, the letters of the time being so few, not much was found. When all was gathered, however, the usual limit for a 'paper' was exceeded, and so a good opportunity seemed to offer for adopting the plan, which should be more used for local history, of giving documents very fully or entirely and so making them tell their own tale, bringing out the actions and actors of the time and their intentions, without doubt or necessity for further reference. Short as the story is, it forms a sequel to that of the Spanish Armada of exactly a century before; and it may also, perhaps, be just noted now, as the papists of to-day have started an organisation with the idea of reviving an interest in the position here seen destroyed.

THE MARCH OF WILLIAM OF ORANGE THROUGH THE COUNTY OF SOMERSET

In 1671, but ten years after the restoration of Charles II., in the face of Protestant England, and during the lifetime of many actors in the late civil war, the king's brother James, Duke of York, startled the nation by announcing himself a papist. Intense agitation ensued. Much debate arose about the succession to the crown, with special reference to the duke's exclusion, it being well understood and publicly argued that a king who is a papist acknowledges thereby that he is not supreme in the land. As to whether the succession could be changed, or how it could be done, there was a difference of opinion. It was to the interest of the kingdom, thought some, that it should continue only in the direct line; these forgetting, said the others, that the king, lords, and commons had a right to dispose of it.

Then there was the question of the duke's marriage. We 'fear we shall have the daughter of Modena for our duchess,' says a letter of this time—a fear which proved to be true. On a proposition being made in the commons, that the marriage should not be consummated, and that the duke should marry a Protestant, the discussion was stopped by the Parliament being at once prorogued. Avoiding too much detail as belonging to the general history of the time, only a few points can be noticed here. The Parliament gone, the king, glady rid of the restraint, chose to violate the constitution, especially by issuing a 'Declaration of Indulgence,' which removed all the penal laws purposely passed against Roman Catholics.

In the spring of 1673 the Parliament again assembled, when immediately this declaration was attacked and its revocation demanded. It was cancelled accordingly, and followed by the Test Act, by which every one holding any office was compelled, under penalty of disqualification, to take oaths of allegiance and supremacy, to deny transubstantiation, and to receive the Sacrament according to the usage of the Church of England. 'What would the duke do?' was the query of the day. It is 'bruited about,' wrote one, 'that he will take, but it is much doubted.' All doubt was soon solved when, finding himself unable to accept the imposed conditions, he was obliged to throw up his appointments. In 1679 this Parliament was dissolved and another elected. The great point with the new house was the bill for the exclusion of the duke from the succession to the crown. Against this the king was ready to promise anything, but no promise would be accepted; the consequence was, first, a prorogation, May 26, 1679, followed soon after by a dissolution. A new election followed in the same year; but, the result going against the king, the Parliament was prorogued without meeting. In October, 1680, when the house met, the Exclusion Bill was again the prominent subject; but, the bill being eventually thrown out by the lords, the king at once dissolved.

Feelings were now very strong; the whole country was in

THE MARCH OF WILLIAM OF ORANGE THROUGH THE COUNTY OF SOMERSET

IN 1671, but ten years after the restoration of Charles II., in the face of Protestant England, and during the lifetime of many actors in the late civil war, the king's brother James, Duke of York, startled the nation by announcing himself a papist. Intense agitation ensued. Much debate arose about the succession to the crown, with special reference to the duke's exclusion, it being well understood and publicly argued that a king who is a papist acknowledges thereby that he is not supreme in the land. As to whether the succession could be changed, or how it could be done, there was a difference of opinion. It was to the interest of the kingdom, thought some, that it should continue only in the direct line; these forgetting, said the others, that the king, lords, and commons had a right to dispose of it.

Then there was the question of the duke's marriage. We 'fear we shall have the daughter of Modena for our duchess,' says a letter of this time—a fear which proved to be true. On a proposition being made in the commons, that the marriage should not be consummated, and that the duke should marry a Protestant, the discussion was stopped by the Parliament being at once prorogued. Avoiding too much detail as belonging to the general history of the time, only a few points can be noticed here. The Parliament gone, the king, glady rid of the restraint, chose to violate the constitution, especially by issuing a 'Declaration of Indulgence,' which removed all the penal laws purposely passed against Roman Catholics.

In the spring of 1673 the Parliament again assembled, when immediately this declaration was attacked and its revocation demanded. It was cancelled accordingly, and followed by the Test Act, by which every one holding any office was compelled, under penalty of disqualification, to take oaths of allegiance and supremacy, to deny transubstantiation, and to receive the Sacrament according to the usage of the Church of England. 'What would the duke do?' was the query of the day. It is 'bruited about,' wrote one, 'that he will take, but it is much doubted.' All doubt was soon solved when, finding himself unable to accept the imposed conditions, he was obliged to throw up his appointments. In 1679 this Parliament was dissolved and another elected. The great point with the new house was the bill for the exclusion of the duke from the succession to the crown. Against this the king was ready to promise anything, but no promise would be accepted; the consequence was, first, a prorogation, May 26, 1679, followed soon after by a dissolution. A new election followed in the same year; but, the result going against the king, the Parliament was prorogued without meeting. In October, 1680, when the house met, the Exclusion Bill was again the prominent subject; but, the bill being eventually thrown out by the lords, the king at once dissolved.

Feelings were now very strong; the whole country was in

a ferment. The position was not unlike that of the time of Charles I.; the unconstitutional proceedings of the king in favour of popery producing a hatred which led to personal armament.

The Protestant religion, said the City of London, was primitive Christianity restored. 'Nobody,' wrote one, 'will trust the Church of Rome further than they can command her. She may be compared to the tiger which fawns, sneaks, and lurks as long as the hunter is armed with his spear and his gun; but, when once the weapons are laid down, the beast flies upon the unwary one and tears and devours him.' All were thus cautioned to be aware, and not to fall victims to the lawless fury and barbarity of such a sort, subtle and treacherous by custom and discipline, not to be chained by any law, either of God or man.[1]

The Parliament being dissolved, the towns sent addresses to their representatives. Some from Somerset were published in a pamphlet under the title of 'Vox Patriæ: Resentments and Indignation of the Free-born Subjects of England against Popery, arbitrary Government, and the Duke of York or any Popish Successor.' Bridgwater, by letter agreed upon by the mayor and inhabitants on February 26, 1681, addressed Sir Halswell Tynte and Sir John Malet:

We greet you both with our most humble and hearty service, and by these inform you that on Saturday, the 26th past, with all becoming calmness and fairness, we elected you to be our burgesses and representatives in the ensuing Parliament.

We do also unanimously approve of that great care and indefatigable industry which the last Parliament took in and

[1] *Modest Vindication of the Petition of the Lords.*

towards the securing the Protestant religion (than which nothing is more dear to us), his Majesty's sacred person and Government, together with the vindication and preservation of our native rights, liberties, and priviledges: for their utmost endeavour to bring the betrayers of the same, together with all the principal conspirators in that most damnable and hellish popish plot, to condign punishment, not omitting our grateful acknowledgements of those many good bills which they had prepared: and, moreover, for all those worthy votes, resolutions, and orders made and past in that most loyal and never-to-be-forgotten Parliament, whereof one of you in the last and both of you in former Parliaments (to our great comfort and encouragement) approved yourselves faithful members.

We do also humbly and heartily desire and petition you to follow their good precedent and example in this ensuing Parliament to do your utmost to secure the king's person, with the Protestant religion (which we apprehend, with deep sense of mind, to be in eminent danger) from all popish attempts and conspiracies whatsoever: as also to take care for the exclusion and prevention of any popish successor from inheriting the imperial crown of this realm.

In the firm and faithful discharge of that great trust we have reposed in you (whereof we do not in the least doubt) withal confidently believing, that you will not charge our estates, till we are effectually secured from popery and arbitrary government; we do assure you that we will stand by you with our lives and fortunes; and we shall ever pray for your good success.

On March 11 Taunton sent its address, as follows, to Edmund Prideaux and John Trenchard, Esqrs.:

Worthy Sirs,

We do most heartily acknowledge your great wisdom, courage, and faithfulness in the discharge of the trust by us reposed in you as members of the late dissolved Parliament, whose worthy endeavours for the happiness of the king and kingdom exceedingly rejoiced the hearts of true English and Protestant spirits, and will make them famous to posterity.

And now, Sirs, having in full assurance of your perseverance in the same good works, we have presumed again to make choice of you as our representatives in the ensuing Parliament, desiring your acceptance of that great trust: and begging you, as that wherein the glory of God, the interest of the Protestant religion, the safety and welfare of the king and kingdom is highly concerned, to prosecute (as shall be guided by the wisdom of that honourable house), these following particulars, viz.:

1. That some effectual course may be taken for the safety of his Majesty's sacred person and Government, which have been and still are in extreme danger by the abominable plots and attempts of papists.

2. That further search made into the horrid popish plot, and the plotters and abettors thereof brought to condign punishment.

3. That you will joyn with the rest of that honourable house (whereof you are now chosen to be members) in repeating the endeavours of the two last worthy Parliaments to bar all papists (and especially James, Duke of York) from the exercise of the royal authority of this kingdom.

4. That you will with all diligence endeavour the uniting of his Majesties Protestant subjects, and the repealing those severe laws that are obstructive thereof.

5. That all good endeavours be used for the securing of

our religion and property, and the just rights and privileges of the subject.

6. That some law may be made for the preventing of the excesses and exorbitancies in the election of members of Parliament, and of undue returns; and that some effectual provision may be made for the meeting of frequent Parliaments, and for their sitting to redress grievances, and to make such wholesome laws as shall be necessary for the welfare of this nation.

7. That some effectual course be taken to give a check to prophaneness and debauchery, which threaten ruine or at least exceeding great prejudice to the kingdom.

In prosecuting of all which worthy acts we shall endeavour your defence with our lives and fortunes.

This was followed by another, clear and plain spoken, showing the strong feeling, and curious as coming from the non-enfranchised. It is:

The Humble Address of the Young Men of the Burrough of Taunton to Edmund Prideaux and John Trenchard, Esquires, who were unanimously chosen by the Inhabitants to be Representatives of the said Borough to serve in this Parliament, which is to sit at Oxford, March 21, 1681–2.

SIRS,

Though we are not immediately concerned in the electing members to serve in Parliament, yet being deeply sensible that we shall bear an equal share with others in the same common danger and universal slavery which hell and Rome have been, and still are, with joint and unwearied endeavours, attempting to involve these Protestant nations in, we cannot without charging ourselves with unparallell'd ingratitude, omit the returning you our hearty thanks for that good and eminent service you did both us and the nation in the late dissolved Parliament. That you did with such inflamed zeal, with such undaunted courage and resolution, endeavour the security of our religion, liberty, and property against that accursed popish faction who were the invaders of them; particularly we deem ourselves infinitely obliged for the great care you manifested in the preservation of his Majesties sacred person, in your strenuous prosecution of the horrid and damnable popish plot, and in that your attempts were so brisk and vigorous for the preventing of an arbitrary and tyrannical power (which we cannot but unanimously abhor), liberty and property being an inheritance which as Englishmen we are born unto. And above all we commend your courage and prudence in prosecuting that happy expedient of excluding a popish successor from inheriting the imperial crown of this realm; without which we judge it utterly impossible that the Protestant religion can be secured to us, or that our necks can be long free from that Romish yoke, which neither we nor our fathers were able to bear; and now, sith it has pleased our gracious king to issue forth his royal proclamation signifying his pleasure to meet his people again in Parliament, we cannot but address ourselves to you, the representatives of this borough, humbly requesting that you would, according to the trust reposed in you, vigorously prosecute those counsels that have a tendency to a happy settlement of affairs both in Church and State; particularly our unanimous request to you is:

1. That forasmuch as the late horrid and hellish plot hath, according to the votes of the preceding Parliaments, received life and countenance from James, Duke of York, you would

expedite a bill for the utter incapacitating him ever to sway the scepter of these kingdoms, and that the Bill of Association may be annexed, whereby all his Majesties subjects may be enabled to oppose him or any of his accomplices in case he should attempt to possess himself of the same.

2. To take such measures as your wisdom shall agree upon for the uniting of the Protestant interest in these nations.

3. That the artillery and militia of the nation be settled in the hands of men of known integrity, courage, and conduct, and that all papists and popishly affected persons now in places of public trust be discharged (which if effected) may be a means to prevent those great fears and jealousies which are apt otherwise to be nourished amongst us.

4. That you proceed to the tryal of popish lords, together with all other criminal offenders, and go on sifting to the bottom that execrable plot which hath been, and we must fear still is carried on, to take away his Majesties life (whom God long preserve) ; to root out the fundamental laws of this realm, as also to introduce popery into the Church and tyranny into the State.

5. That you take cognizance of the illegal and arbitrary proceedings of courts, as well ecclesiastical as civil, as you have begun, that so the laws may not be wrested against the Protestant dissenters, nor stretched in favour of popish recusants, as also to consider the unpresidented finings and imprisonings, whereby many of his Majesties truly loyal subjects have been grievously oppressed.

6. That you would speedily think of some good expedient for the regulating of elections, as also for removing of those oaths and tests which have proved no small hindrance to divers worthy Protestants from being useful instruments in serving their king and country in Church and State. These

things, worthy Sirs, we humbly offer to your considerations, not as directors but remembrancers, out of a principle of loyal zeal for his Majesties security and our countries tranquillity: and assure yourselves in the prosecution of these truly noble designs, we will defend you with our lives and fortunes; accounting our dearest blood a tribute due to the safety of our king and country, when called for in their defence.

The king, too, received addresses from others, with apparently loyal intentions and with expressions of thanks, sometimes rather qualified, for his 'gracious declaration.' Beginning in April, the following came from Somerset:

The Humble Declaration and Address of your Majesties Deputy Lieutenants, Justices of the Peace, and Officers of your Majesties Militia in and for the County of Somerset.

MOST GRACIOUS SOVEREIGN,

We, your Majesties most loyal and obedient subjects of the county of Somerset, whose names are subscribed, being sensible of the great blessings this kingdom has enjoyed under your Majesties government since your Majesties happy restauration thereunto, and having our hearts filled with joy by your Majesties late declaration touching your royal intentions as to the future administration thereof, cannot remain silent, but as a part of the greater body do presume to approach your royal throne with our most humble acknowledgements of your Majesties goodness and clemency expressed unto us in that your Majesties declaration, and particularly for that your Majesty is graciously pleased to give us your royal word that our persons and estates shall not be left to the pleasure of our fellow-subjects. We are deeply sensible of the endeavors that have been on foot to subvert the known laws of the land, wherein our religion, liberty, and property are wound up. And we are so far satisfied that it is the kingdom's interest to continue the succession in its due and right line, and maintain the present government as by law it is established, that we for our own parts are unanimously resolved, by God's help, to assist and serve your Majesty with our lives and fortunes in defence thereof, against all persons and parties that shall appear against it.

An Address of the Mayor, Recorder, Aldermen, and Citizens of your ancient and loyal City of Bath.

DREAD SOVEREIGN,

We the Mayor, Recorder, Aldermen, and Citizens of your antient and loyal City of Bath, having to our great joy seen a confluence of your Majesties good subjects in their several addresses, with all suitable and becoming expressions of duty and loyalty, do now (as early as any other in our affections to your Majesty) cheerfully, unanimously, and with all thankfulness, acknowledge your Majesties great goodness and condescension, in publishing your late gracious declaration, by which we are fully assured of what we can reasonably wish or hope for in all our concerns, both as to our present and future conditions. And we beseech your Majesty to accept, not only of our unfeigned and humble thanks, but also of this assurance from us (which is our bounden duty) that we resolve to stand by your Majesty with our lives and fortunes, in the vindication of your Majesties prerogative, and of those pious resolutions you have expressed to preserve our present established religion, our liberties and properties. The good God bless your Majesties reign with many and happy days, and grant that the Crown may never cease to flourish on the royal head of your Majesty and of your lawful successors, till time shall be no more.

The Humble Address of the Mayor, Aldermen, and Burgesses of your Majesties Town, Borough, and Corporation of Taunton, St. Mary Magdalen and St. James, in your County of Somerset.

We, your Majesties humble, loyal, and obedient subjects, having taken notice of your Majesties gracious declaration, wherein your Majesty is pleased to assure us that the law shall be your guide; so shall we have no need to doubt but the now established government shall continue both in Church and State, whereby the cruelty of Rome with the foxlike dissenters, the moths of the State and the enemies to your gracious goodness, shall receive their condign punishment. We do in all humility render our unfeigned thanks, blessing the King of Heaven for such a blessing in preserving so good a prince as your most royal Majesty, by whose happy restauration we have received the benefit of peace and profit. Notwithstanding the malice of those who are your and our enemies, we are resolved that we shall be ready to make our loyalty appear, for the preservation of your Majesties life and prerogatives, with our lives and fortunes. God grant your Majesty a long and prosperous reign, and that your enemies have no power to hurt you, is the prayer of your Majesties loyal and obedient subjects.

To the Worshipful Sir Edward Philips and the rest of the Worshipful Justices assembled for the keeping the General Sessions of the Peace for this County at Bridgwater, the 12th instant (July), anno regni regis 33, *anno que dom,* 1681.

The presentment of the grand inquest for the said county, holden at the time and place abovesaid.

Imprimis. We present it as our duty to return thanks to the worshipful bench for declaring to the county, that the laws against popery, schisime and faction, conventicling and other unlawful meetings (things highly obnoctious and destructive to the true government) ought to be put in execution; and particularly to those worthy ones of the bench, who in their own persons have given example and laid foundation before us for the punishing such officers as have been remiss in their duty touching the premises.

Item. We present it to be our bounden duty, and in all humble manner, make it our request and prayer to the worshipful bench, that care be taken that we may be recommended to his most gracious Majesty, rendering all imaginable thanks for his most seasonable, suitable and gracious declaration and preservation of the lawful succession, religion and property, supporting the government in Church and State, as anciently, according to the known laws; preserving a godly orthodox ministry which never as yet taught subject to rebel against their lawful sovereign, and for declaring to the world, that as he had not as yet, nor ever would, arbitrarily rule over us, so he would not suffer our fellow-subjects to do the same, of whom great suspicion lately was, since some of them by caballing and other indirect means procured others to carry on a design even against Cæsar himself, prohibiting under a penalty to render him even his due, quite contrary to the precept and example of our blessed Saviour (who though indigent) yet by the hand of another rendered Cæsar his own, by which we plainly perceive specious pretences are not valid, nor may we account such truly religious, but such as are truly loyal. Therefore we humbly pray that his sacred Majesty may be informed hereof, as aforesaid; and that he will persevere in preserving the said succession, religion and property, the establishment of the Church, and bring to condign punishment all its opposers, and not suffer himself to be shipwrack'd under any specious pretences of his and our fatal enemies; and we do hereby assure him to this end that we will not only contribute what our mean fortunes will afford, but will readily sacrifice even our lives to maintain and justifie the same. In testimony whereof we have hereunto put our hands the day and year above written.

The Humble Address of the Mayor, Aldermen, Burgesses, and other Inhabitants of your Majesties ancient and ever loyal Burrough of Axbridge in your County of Summerset.

MOST GRACIOUS AND DREAD SOVEREIGN,

We, your Majesties most dutiful and loyal subjects, being sensibly affected with the great happiness which we have always possessed under your Majesties protection, do in all humility beseech your royal goodness to accept of these our unfeigned acknowledgements of the same. And whereas the restless malice of some ill men hath labour'd to poison your subjects' loyalty with unreasonable jealousies touching your sacred Government (which we can neither harbor in ourselves nor countenance in others) as we believe that your gracious declaration is abundantly sufficient (if well consider'd) to suppress them all, so we do most cheerfully render our thanks for it, being exceeding joyful that thereby your Majesty hath signified your firm resolutions to rule us in all things according to the laws of the kingdom, to advise frequently with your Parliament, to maintain the hereditary right of succession to your crown, and to use your utmost endeavours to extirpate popery. And we do, according to the oaths of supremacy and allegiance by us taken, most solemnly protest before God and the world that no temptation whatever shall hinder us from sacrificing our liberties, lives, and fortunes in defence of your royal person, prerogatives, heirs, and lawful successors against all domestic and forreign attempts to the contrary. And we do and ever shall pray unto God Almighty to preserve long your sacred life in safety, peace, and honour, that you may be always a support unto your friends, and a terror unto your enemies at home and abroad. In testimony whereof we have hereunto put our hands, and affixed our common seal this 4th day of August, in the thirty-third year of your Majesties reign over England, Scotland, France, and Ireland. Ann. Dom. 1681.

It may be remembered here that it was in this year 1681, in the midst of this unrest, the Duke of Monmouth, the Protestant duke, made his well-known progress through Somerset.

Three years passed—the constitutional time for a new Parliament—but it was not called. The king never cared to meet another. In February, 1685, Charles died, and all attempts to exclude the Duke of York having so far failed, he succeeded to the crown as James II.

Not willingly the new king called a new Parliament. When it met on May 19, the question of religion was at once considered, and a demand made for the execution of all penal laws against Nonconformists. Greatly enraged on learning this, James soon showed his intentions to be rid of such interference, as in November he prorogued the Parliament, and, allowing it to remain prorogued, proceeded to attempt a Government without one.

Again, it may be remembered that this year 1685 is marked in Somerset by the rebellion in support of the Duke of Monmouth. Besides the Popish Plot, there was also at this time what one party called the Protestant Plot—this meaning a plan, in addition to excluding the Duke of York, of getting the king to nominate his successor; and from Charles's strong feelings of affection for the Duke of Monmouth it was thought he would name him. But, as the preliminaries did not happen, Monmouth's illegitimacy kept aloof many who could not see the crown descend otherwise than in the direct line, and who moreover knew that, if the queen bore no son, the king's daughters—Mary, wife of the Prince of Orange, and after her Anne, wife of Prince George of Denmark, both Protestants—must succeed by ordinary right. It was therefore only a question of a few years' forbearance, and all would come well.

A year and a half later, in April, 1687, acting on his own sole authority, the king violated all rule and superseded the law, by abolishing the laws against the papists, and especially the tests which had been so recently and so specially aimed at himself when Duke of York, by issuing what was called 'A Declaration of Toleration and Liberty of Conscience.' By this the penal laws for not attending church, or for not receiving the Sacrament, or for nonconformity, were immediately suspended; the king's idea being that the Protestant nonconformists would readily accept and welcome for themselves this great relief, and thus would be aiding him in gaining full liberty for his own co-religionists, the popish nonconformists.

In this, however, he was doomed to disappointment, as, besides that the Protestants, as a rule, declined to be relieved in such company, they foresaw the danger of excusing this great illegality. It was perceived that, the test being abolished, papists would be eligible for Parliament. If the penal laws were repealed, it might be argued that popery was legally re-established; as if, after a law be repealed, such repealing law be in turn repealed unconditionally, the original position must revive. Any promise of an equivalent would, it was well known, in the hands of popery amount to nothing; when a popish Parliament was once obtained, away would go the promise and the equivalent.

Accompanied and covered as they were by the king's pretentious claim to personal authority, these popish contrivances became intolerably vexatious and unbearable. It was necessary, therefore, on behalf of the king, that every effort should be made to obtain support, or at least some appearance of it. Lord Stawell wrote from Ham that he would always use his utmost endeavours to promote the election of sound and loyal members.[1] Judge Jeffreys wrote: 'I shall not be wanting either in my person or purse to serve my master in this or anything else I can be capable of.'[2] Pressure too was brought to bear on local authorities. From Edward Baber, Sheriff of Somerset, came a letter from Bridgwater, February 18, 1686, which shows well what was being done. 'In obedience to his Mats. command,' wrote the Sheriff, ' he had dismist Mr. Steer from the office of Under-Sheriff, though very well assured of his loyalty, which he could have sufficiently shown by the juries he would returne. He (the Sheriff) would take care to pitch upon a person against whom there could be no objection, whose name should be sent up for approval.' He apologised for not answering earlier; but the letter, dated the 6th inst., came not to his hands until Friday last, after it had been twice broken open.[3]

Every effort, too, was made to get addresses sent up approving of the king's conduct; but, after much labour to this end, the success was very small. Those which came were

---

[1] *State Papers, Dom.* 1685, No. 181.   [2] *Ibid.*, No. 82.
[3] *Ibid.*, No. 51.

'very graciously received,' and then ostentatiously printed in the 'London Gazette.' The following is probably a complete list of those from Somerset.

The first in order of date, May 26, 1687, was :—

The Humble Address of divers of your Majesties Dissenting Subjects, on the behalf of themselves and many others, in and near your Town of Taunton in the County of Somerset.

GREAT SIR,

The extraordinary and undeserved favours which your Majesty hath been pleased out of your royal clemency and bounty to confer upon us since the late unhappy rebellion, do oblige us by the strictest ties of duty and gratitude, first to return our most hearty thanks to Almighty God, and next our most grateful and humble acknowledgements unto your Majesty.

Your gracious pardon secur'd many of us, our lives, and all that we do enjoy; and your generous indulgence in matters of conscience hath restor'd to us the freedom of serving our God, without fear or disturbance; which with your Majesties rational presumption of the concurrence of your two Houses of Parliament, with your Royal SELF, in so good and great an undertaking, gives the strongest foundation to our hopes, that liberty and property being thereby secured, peace, prosperity, and ease will flow from hence to your Majesties Dominions, your Majesties gracious proceedings herein, hath laid upon us greater obligations to duty and allegiance, than all the oaths, tests, and subscriptions that could have been imposed. Hereby we have the greatest encouragement to industry in our stations since the penal laws (which prey'd on the vitals of our trade) are taken out of the way. We trust you shall never have cause to repent, that your favours are bestowed on persons disloyal or unthankful: And that we may enjoy many prosperous days under the favourable auspices of your government. But chiefly that all the blessings of Heaven may for ever crown your sacred Majesty. We shall ever pray, &c.

On June 27 appeared :—

The Humble Address of the thanks of several Dissenting Ministers of the Gospel, Inhabitants in the Western Part of the County of Somerset.

GREAT SIR,
    It having pleased your most excellent Majesty in your princely wisdom, and in a tender consideration of the deplorable condition of your Majesties dissenting subjects, who groaned under the penal laws; to emit your most gracious declaration for liberty of conscience, whereby you manifest how much it lies upon your royal heart to establish the quiet, ease, peace, and welfare of all your subjects. We your Majesties most loyal and most dutiful subjects, sharers in this great favour, do, as well in the names of our respective congregations, as in our own, after most humble acknowledgements to Almighty God, in all humility, present your Majesty our most unfeigned and hearty thanks, for the liberty we enjoy by that sovereign act of grace; professing it shall be the care and employment of our whole lives, as it is our duty to answer the great obligations laid upon us thereby; and to meet your Majesties transcendent goodness, in all the methods of a perfect gratitude and chearful obedience. That this foundation of settlement, which your Majesty hath so

wisely laid, may be built upon, to the glory of God, and the happiness of all your subjects: That your Majesty may be blessed with the choicest blessings, both of Heaven and earth, that your reign may be long and prosperous, your Crown flourish, and the glory of it had in remembrance to all generations, shall ever be the prayers and endeavours of,

GREAT SIR,
Your Majesties most humble,
faithful and obedient Subjects.

On August 25 came two addresses from Bath; the first was:—

To the King's most Excellent Majesty.

The Humble Address of several Members of the Corporation, and of other Freemen and Inhabitants of your ancient City of Bath.

MAY IT PLEASE YOUR MAJESTY,

After all our expressions of joy wherewith your Majesty and your royal consort have been welcom'd into this your city; we desire to cast ourselves at your sacred feet, with all dutiful and loyal deference unto your royal pleasure, and undoubted prerogative in publishing your late gracious declaration. We think it, great sir, inconsistent with true piety, or with that loyalty which we, for our parts, have always profest, to repine that the influence of your royal benignity is not confin'd to a party, but (like that of the divine) doth diffuse itself over all your dominions, and that our eye should be therefore evil because your Majesty is good, which princely indulgence, as we do gratefully acknowledge, so will we, in our several stations, whensoever your Majesty shall think fit to issue forth your writs for that purpose, endeavour that such persons be chosen to serve in Parliament as will readily concur with your Majesty in this your compassionate grace and favour to your people. And that by this your unparalell'd act of clemency, all your subjects may be united in their allegiance to their prince, and in love and charity to each other, and your Majesty have an empire in the hearts and affections of your people, divided only with the King of kings, shall ever be the prayer of,

Dread Sovereign,
Your Majesties ever dutiful
and loyal Subjects.

The second was:—

The Humble Address of the High Steward, Mayor, Aldermen and capital Citizens of your Majesties ever loyal City of Bath, in the County of Somerset.

MIGHTY MONARCH,

As soon as the imperial crown descended to your most sacred head, we did, in all humility, return your Majesty our thanks for your gracious declaration, wherein we were then certain of enjoying our religion, rights, and properties. We then assured your Majesty our lives and fortunes stood ready to be engaged in your Majesties service, which, on the first opportunity, we faithfully performed, in defending your Majesties city of Bath against James Scot and his abettors; and our resolutions at that time were so loyally fixt, that we resolved to die at our gates rather than suffer them to come within the walls of your Majesties city, which plainly appeared by killing the first of that party that summoned the city to surrender. And now, great sir, we again return your

Majesty our due and hearty thanks, not only for your gracious favour to us for the enjoying our religion, but for your mercy, clemency, and goodness in pardoning your greatest enemies, hoping that may cure their distracted minds; if not, we, your Majesties loyal subjects of this city, will be always ready to hazard our lives, in defence of your Majesties most sacred person, which that God may always preserve, shall be the prayers of us,

Your Majesties most dutiful and loyal Subjects.

After some interval, on October 10 came:—

The Humble Address of your Majesties poor and loyal Subjects the Combers, Weavers, and other Labourers in the Serge Manufacture in and near your Town of Taunton, in the County of Somerset, on the behalf of our selves, and a multitude of others.

GREAT SIR,

The ease and happiness we enjoy by your gracious influences on us, is such as justly causeth love and admiration in us: you have let your mercy take place of justice, and not only given your generous pardon to us, but freed us from the rapacious hands of those that made a prey of our very labour, and raised their own private fortunes on that which should have fed our wives and children. The benefits which we receive from your goodness is beyond expression, and you have given us opportunity to learn to be good men, by your gracious declaration of liberty of conscience to all your subjects, which we hope will have that effect as will unite the hearts and affections of all your subjects to your self, and one to another; that while interest of parties are laid aside, the common interest, trade and safety of the nation may be advanc'd and promoted by all; that your Majesty, as the common father of your country, may, by your happy councils, live to see this the most peaceable and prosperous nation of the world; and that all your actions may be attended with success and glory, even such as always attends the great, the good, and just; that you may never want the influences of heaven to bestow a thousand fold on you for all your gracious benefits toward us, shall be the constant prayers of your poor, loyal, and dutiful subjects.

This was followed on October 20 by :

The Humble Address of divers of your Majesties loyal Subjects, commonly called Presbyterians, Ministers and others, from their Congregations in the East of Somerset, Bath, Shepton, Froom, Bruton, Wincanton, Milborne, Friary, Inscoomb.

MOST ROYAL SIR,
You have been pleased so freely and admirably to manifest your love to your faithful subjects, by your late most noble declaration of liberty in the worship of God, and in our callings, beyond any of your ancestors, that it would be the greatest ingratitude imaginable, if from our souls and hearts we do not sincerely acknowledge it; we therefore, in all prostrate humility, do render your Majesty our most hearty thanks and service in all the duties of loving, faithful and obedient subjects, for the preservation of your royal person and dignity, who hath most graciously given so much ease to an afflicted people after so long and grievous suffering, and also a new life in the trade and industry of the nation; and we hope that none of your Majesties sincere loyal subjects

ll show dislike in words or behaviour of this your Majesties most deliberate and wise dispensation, and for our parts, whose names are hereunto subscribed, multitudes of our neighbours consenting with us, we do joyfully embrace your Majesties favour and gracious promises made unto us.

The next, and last, from Chard, October 22, marks a pretty episode in local history :—

To the King's Most Excellent Majesty.

We, your Majesties most loyal and most dutiful subjects, the portreeve, burgesses, principal freeholders, and others the inhabitants of your Majesties borough of Chard in the county of Somerset, being weary with waiting to see the address from the Corporation of Mayor and Justice, &c., in the said borough, presume now to present your Majesty with this our following humble address the 22nd of October, 1687.

GREAT SIR,
   The good effects that your Majesties most gracious declaration hath had both on the persons and estates of your Majesties subjects are so visible that none can or dare deny the good influence thereof, but such as are biassed by a principle of disloyalty towards their prince, and malice towards their fellow subjects ; and therefore, for our parts, (though we know your Majesty to be far above our acknowledgements, or promises, yet) reflecting upon the Egypt your Majesties tender-conscienced subjects were in, the cruel task-masters they served under, and possessing the Canaan you have been pleased to conduct them to, we cannot suffer the heathen to upbraid us, from whom we have it as a maxim, *Si*

ingratum dixeris, omnia dixeris. But we presume to lay our selves down at your Majesties feet, rendering our most unfeigned thanks for your gracious declaration of liberty of conscience, promising all faithful loyalty and our utmost endeavours in the several stations and capacities in which God hath set us under our sovereign, that there shall be such representatives elected (whenever it shall be your royal pleasure to call a Parliament) as shall answer your expectation, remove both the penal laws and test and enact your kingly declaration into a perpetual law, to which we heartily add

God save the King and say Amen.

The curious position suggested by this address must be explained. Chard, in A.D. 1234, received certain liberties from the bishop as then lord of the manor, one being that the superintendence of the town, hitherto done by the bishop's steward as his nominee, was transferred to a chief elected by the burgesses, who became thus the portreve. Some time about 1570 the town appears to have been incorporated under a mayor, when the office of portreve would cease. This charter, not now to be found, was forfeited in 1662, as the corporation did not appear to be sufficiently loyal to the newly restored king, or rather to his attempt to enforce uniformity in religion. After this forfeiture the old system with the portreve was resumed, Chard under him remaining true to nonconformity. Time having passed, and the stronger feelings having presumably softened somewhat, the conformist party, under the influence of Lord Paulet, the new lord of the manor, promoted and obtained a new charter in 1683, thus reviving the mayoralty. This attempt of the Tory party to obtain precedence led to a curious position, as the other party in possession adhered to the old system under a portreve and declined to be superseded. Thus one party elected a mayor, the other a portreve, the two chiefs actually existing at the same time. It was then the nonconformists, 'weary with waiting for some sign' from the mayor and his party, who sent up this address, perhaps rather in opposition to the mayor than as being really thankful for an indulgence not enacted 'into a perpetual law.'

When such addresses are got up contrary to the feeling of the nation, especially when attempted for the crown against a Parliament, they can never be of any weight. As a rule now they were got up by, and contained only the sentiments of a few interested persons who really deceived the king. Many who thus gave thanks had no vote, were entirely without influence, and of no consideration. The numerous addresses to Richard Cromwell but a short time before may be remembered. Of the many hundred thousands who in that way vowed to live and die for him, not one drew a sword when he was set aside.

The king's declaration said that he could not but heartily wish that all his people were of the Catholic Church: to this the Epicureans answered:—

No party is more advanced by your indulgence than we are, as the nation must by toleration be freed of the troublesome bigotries of religion. Your Majesty was pleased to wish that all your subjects were of your own religion, and perhaps your subjects wish that you were of theirs. We can easily swallow a wafer deity, and never cavil at a sacrifice which is unintelligible, nor with the Church of Rome always so indulgent for money. We wish however that the pope would free the world of the fear of hell and devils, of the inquisition and dragoons.

Persistently ignoring all the grumbling and discontent around him, resolving to maintain the declaration, James determined in December to 'revise,' as he called it, the lists of deputy-lieutenants and justices, that those only should be continued who would be 'ready to aid in the accomplishment' of his design, and such others added to them 'from whom a like concurrence and assistance could be expected'; especially were corporations and boroughs, as being the strongholds of advanced opinions, to be 'remodelled,' or their charters forfeited.

No address appears to have come from Bridgwater: as a consequence, it was one of the first to be remodelled. The Privy Council minutes give us some information, showing how the attempt was made. In this month of December the Council minutes record that :—

Whereas by the charter granted to the town of Bridgewater in the county of Somerset a power is reserved to his Majesty by his order in councill to remove from their imployment any officer in the said town, his Majesty in councill is pleased to order, and it is hereby ordered, that William Masey, John Rogers, William Symons, Robert Baker, William Criddle, John Curry and Robert Reeves, capitall burgesses, be, and they are hereby, removed, and displaced from their aforesaid offices in the said town of Bridgewater.

(Signed) WILLIAM BLATHWAYT.

JAMES R.

Trusty and well beloved, we greet you well. Whereas we have by our order in councill thought fit to remove William Masey, John Rogers, Robert Baker, William Criddle, John Curry and Robert Reeves from being capitall burgesses of that our burrough of Bridgewater, and William Symons from being one of the capitall burgesses and towne clerke of the same, we have thought fit hereby to will and require you forthwith to elect and admit our trusty and welbeloved John Gilbert senior, Robert Balche, Roger Hoare, Thomas Turner, Samuel Pitman and John Francklin to be capitall burgesses, and William Bicknell to be one of the capitall burgesses and towne clerke of our said burrough in the room of the persons above mentioned without administering unto them any oath or oathes but the usual oath for the execution of their respective places with which we are pleased to dispense in this behalfe, and for so doing this shall be your warrant. Given at our Court at Whitehall 6th day of December 1687 in the third year of our reigne.

By his Majesty's command,
SUNDERLAND.

Following this the charter was forfeited and surrendered, this being the only case in Somerset where a surrender was actually completed and enrolled.

These proceedings produced an increased anxiety on both sides. Books and pamphlets prejudicial to the church and the king were sold on every stall, cried about by hawkers in the streets as commonly as gazettes, and thrown or brought into houses, or sent by penny post in bundles.[1] So influential were these pamphleteers, that on February 10 a proclamation was issued for suppressing all such 'malignant publications, sold by hawkers and pedlars, framed to amuse and disturb the people's minds.' Disobedience was to be met by 'such punishment as by our prerogative may be inflicted.'

The Parliament, prorogued as already noted in November 1685, was dissolved on July 2, 1687, and before another could

[1] Gutch, *Collectanea Curiosa*, vol. i. p. 326.

be safely called it was necessary that its vote in support of the king should, if possible, be secured. Through the lord-lieutenants of counties, as well as by private reports, the king sought accordingly to learn the bias of the leading men. The following 'Three Questions' were thus privately issued to the county gentry, and others likely to aspire to a seat in Parliament. Every such aspirant was asked :—

1. If in case he shall be chosen knight of the shire or burgess of a towne, when the king shall think fitt to call a Parliament; whether he will be for takeing off the penall laws and the tests.

2. Whether he will assist and contribute to the election of such members as shall be for takeing off the penall laws and tests.

3. Whether he will support the king's declaration for liberty of conscience, by living freindly with those of all perswasions, as subjects of the same prince and good Christians ought to do.

The following answers of the justices and others were returned [1] :—

The late new deputy-lieutenants, whose appointments were not at the time confirmed by the king, are placed as justices of the peace, all of them being in the commission.

The Lord Fitzharding, deputy-lieutenant, consents to all three questions, provided that the Church of England be by any way secured of being maintained.

Francis Paulet, deputy-lieutenant, consents to all the three questions.

Sir William Basset, deputy-lieutenant, consents to all the three questions.

[1] Rawlinson MSS., Bodleian.

William Clark, barrester, consents to all the three questions.

Henry Walrond consents to all the three questions.

Richard Cross consents to the two first questions in what concernes the Roman Catholicks, but will not be ingaged as to the dissenters. Consents to the third question.

Peter Reynon answers that he is too old to act any way, but his opinion is to submitt to what the king thinks fitt to be done.

William Helier, late deputy-lieutenant, consents to the first question soe that the Church of England be by any way secured of being maintained. Answers to the second question, that he will promote the elections of the best men he knowes. Consents to the third question.

William Lacye, late deputy-lieutenant :—That being very decrepit, he is not able to serve the king in Parliament, but consents to the second and third questions.

Henry Bull answers to the first question, that he beleeves he shall give his vote, that the penall laws and tests should be taken away, but desires not to be engaged before he hears the debates. To the second question, that he will endeavour the electing of the fittest men he can. Consents to the third question.

Sir William Portman, Sir Edward Wyndham, Sir Hasewell Tynte, Sir Francis Warre, Sir John Smith, Francis Lutterell, George Horner, Thomas Wyndham, John Piggot, Nath. Palmer (late deputy-lieutenants), and Sir Edward Phelips, answer to the first question that they know not how they may change their opinion upon hearing the debates, but at present are not for takeing away the tests and penall laws. They refuse the second question; consent to the third.

John Prowse (late deputy-lieutenant), John Ashford, James

Cade, answer to the first and second questions, they do not think themselves sufficient judges in this matter, therefore will not be any way engaged. Consent to the third question.

Edward Gorges (late deputy-lieutenant), John Sanford, John Hunt, answer to the first question that they know not what they shall do till they hear the debates. To the second question, that they will promote the elections of the fittest men they can. Consent to the third question.

John Bayley, chancellour, desires not to be obliged to declare himselfe, his subsistance depending cheifly on the churchmen.

Edward Berkeley (late deputy-lieutenant), Joseph Langton, desire time to consider.

Richard Morgan, Edmund Wyndham, answer that they will not consent to the two first questions; but consent to the last.

Doctour Bathurst, Sir Thomas Wyndham, Sir Edward Nevill, Edward Nevill, William Player, Hugh Tynte, were absent.

John Blewet, Doctour Holt, William Symes, Ferrers Greisly, being very sick, could not give any answer.

Thomas Littleton, George Hussey, John Brent, Robert Brent, catholicks, already in the commission of the peace.

Then follows a list of: Catholicks and Dissenters proposed to be added to the commission of the peace in divers parts of the county of Somerset, and some of them to be both justices of the peace and deputy-lieutenants.

Sir Thomas Bridges, of Kensham, to be a deputy-lieutenant; Henry Bridges, of Wells, to be a deputy-lieutenant; John Harrington, near Bath; George Clark, of Swanswick, near Bridgewater; Sir Charles Carteret, near Milborne

Port; William Coward, of Wells; William Strode, near Glastonbury; Edward Strode, near Shepton Mallet, to be a deputy-lieutenant; Edward Clarke, of Chipsley, near Taunton, to be a deputy-lieutenant; George Musgrave, of Nettlecombe, near Mynehead; John Speak, eldest son to George Speak, near Illchester and Evill.

Robert Syderfin, Baldwin Malet, Warwick Bamfeild, John Anthill, a catholick, Charles Steynings, to be deputy-lieutenants.

Glancing at these answers, those rather favourable appear first on the list; then come the 'late' D.-L.'s, whose more decided replies make their intentions clear.

The gentry thus disposed of, a report was obtained, sent up December 20, of the probable action or bias of the boroughs, as follows. The return is entitled :—

An account of the Corporations and other Burrows of the County of Sommerset, and of those persons who are for takeing off the Penall Laws and Tests, and who have interest to be chosen Parliament men, if in some of the Corporations such persons are removed and others in their places as they have already, or shall propose.

Bath.—Will not choose any but such as shall be approved of by the king, soe there will need noe change in that corporation.

My Lord Fitzharding and S^r. William Basset served in the last Parliament.

Wells.—The committee of elections have sometimes admitted members chosen by the major, aldermen, and burgesses only; and sometimes members chosen by the whole towne.

S^r. Tho. Bridges, Henry Bridges and M^r. Coward have a good interest there, and two of them will be probably chosen by the corporation if purged, and returned if there be a good major.

Bridgewater.—It hath allwayes been disputed by the magistrates and the populace who should have the right of choosing burgesses. S^r. John Bawden, lately made alderman of London, hath a sufficient interest to be chosen here. This corporation must be totally altered.

Taunton.—The burgesses are chosen by the whole towne.

Edward Clark of Chipley may be probably chosen there. If John Trenchard be pardoned, he and whom he shall propose to stand with him for the towne will be chosen.

This corporation must be totally altered.

In the three following burrows, the burgesses are chosen by all the inhabitants, and a certain number of bayliffs, who also returne them. The office of bayliff depends not on the king, but belongs to the lords of certaine mannors.

Ilchester.—M^r. W^m. Strode will certainely be chosen there. W^m. Rodland, alderman of London, may probably be chosen with him.

Mynehead.—Francis Lutterell (who will not comply) hath soe much interest there, that it will be difficult to oppose him. Robert Syderfin, a barrester, hath a good interest, and John Speak if he be not chosen for the county.

Milbourne Port.—Sir Charles Carteret hath the best interest of any one to be chosen in this burrow, & beleevs himselfe able to hinder any one to be chosen with him, who will not comply, especially if John Hunt & Henry Bull be put out of the commission of the peace, which was the only interest that made them be chosen there the last Parliament.

S^r. John Sydenham and John Speak, eldest son to George Speak, do intend to stand for the county, but it is uncertain whether they will be chosen.

Out of these proceedings, and the strong political feeling now dominant everywhere, arose the following curious episode. As the story is better told entirely, the documents are here fully reproduced.

The first is a letter from Edward Strode, high sheriff, complaining of some justices and their opposition to him at Quarter Sessions.[1] The letter is dated Jan. 14, 1688, and shows well the animus of the gentry, as well as the dining customs of the time.

S^r,—I servd ye late under sheriff wth his writ of discharge ye 19th of dec^{ber} past, & ye 2^d of this instant I went to my first county court att ilchester expecting to have mett ye late sheriff ther to have had ye Goale Rolls, writts & all other things belonging to my office turnd over to me according to ye tenour of ye s^d writ yt soe I might have made a keeper & have had a safe place for prisoners, & have been secured for escapes; but ye sheriff never mett me. I found all ye people att ye place, being attorneys & ye rich sober country freeholders (except ye late undersheriff), very well sattisfyed & thankfull for his maties grace in giving present lyberty & designing ye taking off ye penall laws & test. Publicly att ye table I convinced all of ye aboundant kindnes of his matie to his people in his labouring for it. Ye 10th instant I also went to the quarter sessions held at Bruton (because I heard of noe new comission of ye peace seald) to give my attendance on ye justices doubting their mallice ag^t me

[1] Rawlinson MSS.

because of his maties imploying of me & hopd I should have found all things well & easy espetially it being ye lord ffitzhardings town & he ther; but I found ye quite contrary. Y^e first man I discourst was y^t lord who told me his answer to ye lord Walgrave on ye questions proposed by him and y^t wch ye lord Walgrave told him, y^t his matie would secure all ye laws to his people as to their liberty & property, y^t he should answer him y^t he could not be done unlesse his matie would hang eleven judges. He after shewd me and Justice Hunt (a most violent man) a letter from ye lord Walgrave wherein my lord writ him yt his last answer was approvd of by the king & ye others yt answerd negatively to ye questions rejected be sworn. He gave ye lord Walgrave noe other answer but y^t he would first see ye laws securd before ever he would assent or act towards ye taking off ye penall laws & tests & made himself very pleasant. The next thing he talkt wth me about was yt he would see ye panell of ye grand jury. I told him they were all substantiall freeholders & good men & y^t ye under sheriff had ye panell. He sent for ye undersheriff to bring it to him (this was all att an inne) (a very unusuall thing) wⁿ he had it he caused Edward Cleark ye master of ye inne to read ye names & give his character as they were read & he could not object ag^t any only ye old usuall jury weer left out wch troubled ye lord & he would have had me returnd others some of his neighbors, wch I refused to doe. Then he was angry and told me I had returnd a grand jury yt would make an addresse. I told him I thought soe & it was fitt they should for ye king's love to his people. In some short time Sr Edward Phillips came who was sent for by ye lord to hold ye sessions wth Mr Hunt, Mr Thomas Windham, the Chancellor of Wells, Dr Bayly, & Mr Bull. They went to ye hall and after my under sheriff had deliverd them ye precept & ye panell of ye grand jury, David Trim (tho he knew I had espetiall outlawry ag^t him) appeard as deputy clerk of ye peace & in affront to his maties writ he first calld ye bayliffs of the hundred for their hundred juries & as he read them to be sworn those y^t weer sober honest men he would stand up and acquaint ye l^d ffitzharding & Sr Edward Phillips &c. of them to ye great discouragement of them & others, soe for ye grand jury who weer much sleighted & discountenanced by ye court espetially ye lord ffitzharding who talkt with Mr James Tucker ye foreman of ye grand jury to hinder an addresse. His maties writ of outlawry being deliverd me, and Mr Trim in presence, it would have been an escape in me if he weer not taken on it: soe I orderd one of my bayliffs w^n ye court was up to go & serve him wth ye warrant, wch he civilly did noe body taking notice of it. The justices came to ye inne to diñer when wher I was wth ye Duke of Southampton & Mr Speaker Seymour, w^n ye lord ffitzharding came into ye room he came angryly to me and told me that I had returnd a grand jury of purpose to addresse and y^t ye king had not made me sherriff for nought and more to this purpose. I answerd him y^t whilst his matie thought me fitt to serve him I would doe him all faithfull service. We went to diñer wher I was sufficiently abusd & teasd by them having noe body ther of the kings side wth me, but I took courage and did answer them again wthout fear. Presently after diñer news came y^t Trim was arrested. Immediately ye lord ffitzharding, Mr Hunt, but espotially Mr Thomas Windham fell upon me in a most violent mañer & usd me very reproachfully & askt me how I durst one of their officers. Mr Windham was soe furious y^t he talkt of cutting my throat, & I veryly believe if one had not stept between us, he would have struck me, & told me Mr Trim was his officer, meaninge he being recorder of wells & he his towne clerk & I should have askt his leave & given him notice. I vallewd none of them but stood my ground tho single & told them I would never be ashamd to execute the king's writs as long as he should comand & think mee worthy. Att last w^n they saw I would not discharge Trim they p^d down £20 & ye lord ffitzharding, Mr Windham, Mr Stocker, Mr Twiford, all of a sort, became bound for ye other £24. This being over I considerd wth myselfe, if I should stay ye court would take some occasion ag^t me (as afterwards they did) soe I left my under sheriff to wait on them & went home. I was noe sooner gone & they gone to court but they contrivd one Plumer, a hundred bayliffe of ye lord ffitzharding's, who is lord of Bruton hundred, to fall out wth a bayliffe of mine (who was sworn to attend and keep the grand jury) then in ye hall & said aloud y^t was one of Strode's rogues, meaninge me; the other only answerd y^t he should hold his peace for ye time was now over for ye setting up of head & quarters. Upon this ye lord ffitzharding, Mr Windham, Sr Edw. Phillips, & Mr Hunt fell most outrageously upon my bayliffe, s^d y^t he disturbd ye court comanded him to find suerties or they would comitt him. He modestly answerd y^t he did not disturb ye court but answerd him y^t abusd him & prayd their pardon & that he had noe suerties. All would not doe but he should be comitted & now they thought they had gaind their point, soe they comitted him to one Daw, y^t is ye late sheriffs underkeeper, who took him away & kept him till about 7 or 8 o'clock y^t night & then (as I think) by their own contrivance one from the court came to him & told him he might goe about his busines ye court had nothing to say to him. All this while ye court knew I had no goale nor keeper because ye late sheriff had not according to his writ turnd over ye goale to me. This was Tuesday night. Wensday when Sr Edward Phillips & ye rest knew certainly y^t my bayliff was gone out of town (now is their revenge for my causing Trim to be arrested) they calld for my bayliff into court (his name is William Strode); answer was made y^t he was gone out of town. Immediatly ye court, Sr Edward Phillips being ye spoaks man with most outragious fury yt he foamd att ye mouth, find me a hundred pounds and did use such reproachful abusive language agt me y^t it is not fitt to be usd to a footman much lesse to one y^t his matie hath thought fitt to be the sheriff of his county & it is not me but his matie throw me they doe affront. I hope his matie will consider of it, he doth use to maintain his servants. S^r ye busines of this q^{tr} sessions would have been as easyly dispatcht in 2 dayes as in 4, but because Bruton is ye lord ffitzharding's town & Edward Cheek ye master of ye inne wher ye justices doe eat & drink the busines is prolonged to keep ye country men in town to spend their monys & to spend the king's mony for ye justices have each 4^s a day & yt ye king might not have fines to pay it they have this sessions find none yt have been found guilty, some but 6^d, some but 1/^{s}, for greater offences then formerly in other sheriffs times they have fined them 5 marks & 5 pounds. All shews their hearts. They goe to ye hall about 10 o'clock stay 2 hours then dine and drink well till 4 or 5 and then mazd headed goe to ye hall againe & ther vent their follys ag^t all y^t will not doe like them. S^r if ther be not some notice taken of these things & they sent for to answer it before his matie in counsell, wher I will maintaine what I write to their heads, by wch it will appear they are fitt to be put out of their comissions besides their evill stubbornnes, & it will cleer ye king's justice w^n their crimes are made publick; & if it be not now soe done if his matie thinks fitt to call a Parliament they will soe word beat & brow beat his officers & friends y^t his maties service cañot be preservd, nor right take place. S^r I have thought of a way w^n his matie shall please to call a Parliam^t y^t in every county sober concurring men, such as his matie shall think fitt shall be legally chosen & not misse 2 in 10. But I have allready been too tedious wth a person of y^r great employm^ts, soe will not att present further trouble you wth y^t method nor wth ye names for comissioners of ye sewers wch in y^r letter rec^d you desire, only to y^t p^t about Mr Trim ye persons yt heard him cañot be perswaded to make affidavit being yet under fear, ther being noe new comission, but will justify it on occasion. I hope you will pardon this prolixity, it is out of a dutyfull thankfull zeale for his maties & kingdome's service. Pray keep me in his maties good esteem & what he shall please to command me, to my best understanding shall be performed by,

      S^r y^r most humble servant,
          EDWARD STRODE.
Jany. 14, 1688.

The persons whose names are enclosd you may confide in for Bath.

This letter was answered by the next document, which unfortunately is both unsigned and undated, and bears only the endorsement, Golden Balls, Gerrard Street. In all probability it was from Lord Fitzharding.

That I may give you a satisfactory as well as just relation of what hapned betweene the high sheriff of Somersett, Mr Edward Stroode, and some justices of the peace of the same county at the Quarter Sessions, the tenth of January at Brewton, I must take my rite some yeares before, and acquaint you that after Monmouth's rebellion, when every honest heart was full of detestation of those vile miscreants who had bin the loss of soe many lives & so much treasure in that country, noe person was more zealous to discover those traytors than one David Trim of Wells, who in his search found the aforesaid Mr. Stroode to have abetted it, by giving a considerable sume of without any compultion to Monmouth, this as a good subject he revealed, which made Strood to be seized, who had not now bin sheriffe, had not his maty in great mercy given him his life. This by the sequel seemes plainly to be the foundation on which his spleen is built, for a writt coming into his hand against Trim when he might easily have taken him any day, he reserved it till he could take his revenge the most disgracefully to him & his friends publikely before the county at the sessions, where he knew he must be the clerke of the peace's deputy. This the gentlemen conceived was an affront done to the court, and told him so with very little heate, nor would they protect him which they thought they might, finding by his insolent carriage he sought a quarrell. All they did was to be bound for the debt, every body there thinking this had bin an end of all before in dispute, & that he was satisfied now as well with those who had any warme discourse with him, as with such with whom there had passed nothing but civility & respect. For my owne part I never exceeded those bounds, and doe sweare I thought we had parted loving neighbours. In the afternoon when the sheriff was gon there hapned an accident that might be soe misrepresented that he might be concerned at it. When the grand jury had received their charge, a bayliffe as usually was appointed to waite on them; the jury instead of him appointed desired one Stroode a kinsman of the sheriff's might be the man, which we readily assented to. As soone as in office he called to the other bayliffe as loude as all in the hall heard him, and in an insolent tone, that time of hanging & quartering is over, which being all scandalised at, as a great reflextion on the justice of the nation, we comitted him to the undersheriffe who suffered him to scape, on which we fined the sheriff a hundred pounds, but on his coming in next morning acknowledging his fault the fine was struck off; possibly he was netled at this. If any heate of words passed betweene him & other gentlemen, who have ever bin as eminently loyall as he & his ffamily have been otherwayes, I never knew my country famed for good breeding. To be called before the king & councell will be a punishment will breake their hearts, to find him preferred to them who on all occasions have ventured life & fortune for his Maty, of which I can give many eminent instances. For my owne part I can never be repaired, he hath blasted me in the country, where far from court I desired only leave to pray for the king, which I doe, publicly faithfully & fervently twice a day at least. Then to be cited to appeare before the councell on the bare allegations of a man whose father was so eminent a rebell, he had a particular proclamation to proclaim him so, and he plundred my ffather in the beginning of the rebellion 1642: whose brother carried on a petition to exclude his present Maty, which I put a stop to first of any man in England & turned the streame quite the other way, as my Lord Godolphin well enough knowes. If I have done anything amiss to the king twas for this Stroode, swayed too much by a tender nature, though it did little I often interceded with his Maty to save him, for which I humbly ask God Almighty, the king & countryes pardon. This is all, on my reputation; a little loude, it may be unmannerly, language might pass, and if he had not bin galled he would have winced no more then others.

In reply to this Strode drew up a formal general statement of complaint, as contained in the following fourteen charges.

1. The Lord Fitzharding, telling his answer to the Lord Waldgrave when his lordship told him that his Matie would secure all the laws to his subjects; said that could not be done unless his Matie would hang up eleven judges.

2. The said Fitzharding's answer the second time to the Ld Walgrave, when he proposed to him if he would assist in the takeing of the penall laws & test, that he would not assist nor contribute anything towards it unless the laws were first secured.

3. The Ld Fitzharding desired the sheriffe to return other men for the grand jury, and told him he had returned those men on purpose to make an adress, and endeavoured with the foreman to hinder the makeing an addresse to his Matie. And Mr Hunt the same, as the foreman informed the sherriffe.

4. The Ld Fitzharding told the sheriffe that the king had not made him sherriffe for nothing, and Mr Seymour answered, noe you may be shure the king hath not made him sherriffe for nought.

5. The great abuse offered the sherriffe att dinner, using very unhandsome languige, and said that the feare of hanging made men loyall, and gave them preferment to Mr Hunt (&) Mr Windham. Upon Mr Trym's being arrested on an outlawry Mr Windham came in great fury to the sheriffe & said if he were in another place he would cut his throat & breake his neck downe staires & offered to strike the sherriffe.

(In the margin is written—John Parfitt to prove this.)

7. Mr Hunt came up to the sherriffe in a very furious maner and askt him how he durst arrest one of their offecers and highly threatened the sherriffe.

8. Sr Edward Phillips stood by, whose passion was soe great that he ccould not well speake more then that Mr Tryme was their offecer and should be defended, or words to that purpose.

9. Anthony Stocker, Esqr. & Captaine Twyford stood by all the while & highly opposed the sherriffe and tooke part with Mr Tryme & the justices & presently after went downe into the court & swore God damme the sherriffe, we will doe him some private mischeife.

(Marginal note :—Will Strode to prove this.)

10. Sr Edward Phillipps & the rest sent for Mr Tryme when he was in the bayliffs custody, and when he was come into the roome to them fower offered to be bound for him for twenty fower pounds. Collonel Windham said David Tryme doe Ned Strode what mischeife you can or any that belong to him and I will let thee have a hundred pounds to doe it, and we will all stand by thee, thou shalt not want for freinds, or words to this purpose.

(Note :—Wm Strode to prove this.)

11. Ld Fitzharding, Sr Edward Phillipps, Coll: Windham, Mr Hunt, notwithstanding Mr Tryme was under arrest and outlawd, carried him away with them to the hall from the bayliffs and there ordered him to act the businesse of the sessions and made the bayliff waite till the court did rise for lunch.

(Note :—John Parfitt to prove this.)

12. The Ld Fitzharding's bayliffe of the hundred, one William Plumer, fell out with the sherriffs bayliffe, William Stroud, in the hall & called him one of the sherriff's rogues

and because the said Stroud answered him he was noe such person, and some other words, Sr Edward Phillips and all the bench stood up and said Strod disturbed the court, though they were then about noe businesse, and required him to find shureties or they would committ him. He humbly told them he did not disturbe the court, only answered Plumer, and begged their pardon. However, they committed him to one Robert Daw, one of the late sherriff's goalers & kept him prisoner till 7 or 8 of the clock that night, and then one came & said he came from the justices, & that the said Strode might goe about his businesse, upon which the goaler left him and Strode went out of towne home. The next morning when Sr Edw. Phillipps & the rest heard he was gone out of towne, they had him called in court and on his not appearing, the court fined the sherriffe a hundred pounds tho Strod was never committed to him. The aforsed Plumer said publickly that the king had made Strode sherrif of purpose to doe mischief.

(Note :—Wm Strode to prove this.)

13. Mr Tryme writt severall letters to justices of the peace and deputy-leiveten^{tes} that they should not comply with the Ld. Walgrave to his mat^{ies} proposalls & sent a messenger about with the letters.

14. Mr Tryme when att the sessions he called over the hundred jury & grand jury, if he came to any man's name that he knew was thankfull for his ma^{ties} liberty he would stand up and acquaint Sr Edward Phillipps & the rest with it, who would then frowne upon them and greatly discourage.

(Note :—Wm Strode to prove both these.)

This episode relating to Strode is certainly remarkable, almost incredible, the antecedents attached to the name being remembered. When, in 1628, the Speaker was held down by violence in the chair as he was about to leave it by previous order of the king, rather than record an adverse vote, one of the actors in the scene was William Strode of Devon, member for Beeralston, a turbulent spirit who suffered at this time a harsh and long imprisonment of eleven years. On his release he was again elected, and was next one of the five members accused of treason in January, 1642. On his death in 1645 he had a public funeral, the House attending.

Another William Strode, of Street and Barrington, was prominent in Somerset in opposition to the tax called Ship money. He, with his son, was in the first encounter at Shepton Mallet in August, 1642, and again a few days later, when the very first blood drawn in the civil war was shed on the Polden Hills. As Colonel William Strode he was active through the first years of the war until superseded by the rules of the New Model in 1645. In 1645 he was elected member for Ilchester, and, after a chequered career, died in 1666.

Another William, son of the last-named, entertained the Duke of Monmouth at Barrington on his progress through Somerset in 1681; and in 1685, when the duke was in open rebellion, to prevent a repetition of this, he was seized a day or two after the duke landed at Lyme.[1] This must have been a great loss to Monmouth, but probably it saved Strode's life and estate. He was one of the specially excepted from pardon as William Strode of Street, in the proclamation of March 10, 1685. At what price it was obtained cannot be stated, but he was eventually pardoned by the influence of the Earl of Sunderland, by patent dated July 15, 1687, just after the dissolution of the Parliament.[2] The brother of this William was Edward

---

[1] Roberts's *Life of Monmouth*.
[2] Patent Rolls. House of Lords MSS.

Strode of Downside, in Shepton Mallet, who, on Monmouth's first arrival at Shepton in 1685, contributed to his necessities and gave him a hundred pounds; a goodly sum then; and on his second arrival, when fleeing from Sedgemoor, Monmouth slept his first quiet sleep at Edward Strode's at Downside. Yet with all this precedent not only is William Strode pardoned, and then restored as a deputy-lieutenant, but Edward is put in the special commission of James, and, going over from his old principles to aid this king, is actually made high sheriff in 1687, the very year of his brother's full pardon. That the county gentlemen should be opposed to and disgusted with such an appointment is not surprising. Well may they say it was the fear of hanging that had made Strode loyal.

Another William Strode, the son of Jeffry of Shepton Mallet, was almost a sufferer in the popish plot. Being a prisoner in the King's Bench, he entered into a correspondence with a priest, also a prisoner there, who, having a good opinion of Strode, invited him to his chambers to drink, and so initiated him into the popish plot, to which Strode pretended to agree. But the priest presently 'harboured a jealousie in his thought' that Strode was 'not true to the design,' and so 'began to cast about to ruin him' by causing suspicion to fall upon him.[1]

It is curious, in connection with this name, that a William Strode of Kent, in 1483, 1 Ric. III., was charged with treason as having 'falsely and traiterously ayenst the duete of his ligeaunce assembled greate nowmbre of people harnessed and arraied in manner of werre.'

Besides the returns noticed, others were obtained by special emissaries as to the prospects for the Parliament in the various boroughs. Nathaniel Wade, John Jones, and

[1] Dangerfield's second narrative.

Richard Andrewes, who visited Somerset and Devon, reported that:

Pursuant to your Majesties commands some of our number with others their associates have visited severall corporations and burroughs that elect Members of Parliament.

They had discovered all sorts of men, as to his Maties intentions. Many of the Church of England moderate, their religion being secured according to the declaration; and so with the Presbyterians.

The Roman Catholics, Independents, Anabaptists, and Quaquers, that are numerous in many places, are generally in your Maties interest, notwithstanding many rumours to create jealousy among them.

Monsr Fagell's and other pamphlets are spread through all parts to prejudice those inclined to your Mat^{ie}. Pamphlets to the contrary have been sent down and disperst with good effect. [Fagel's pamphlet, printed in Amsterdam, was: 'A Letter to Mr Stuart, giving an account of the Prince and Princess of Orange's thoughts concerning the Repeal of the Test and Penal Laws.']

Correspondents had been chosen and settled in all counties, corporations, and burroughs, so that they would be kept quickly and truly informed of all matters relating to the election.

The revenue officers they found did not use their influence for his Matie, on the contrary, the post masters were utterly averse thereto.

They thought the returns generally would show a favourable majority.

Somerset.—The county intends to choose Sir John Sydenham and George Speake, or William Stroud and Sir

Thomas Bridges; these are all right. Sir John Sydenham and George Speake have a great interest. The sheriffe desires to know your Majesties pleasure which of those you would have chosen.

Bath.—Is a Corporation; the election is by the body corporate, who propose to choose Oliver Nicholas, one of the Corporation; and Sr William Bassett; who are both right, but if y^r Majesty be not satisfied with those they will choose such as y^r Majesty will recommend.

Wells.—Is a Corporation; the election was allway by the magistrates and burgesses; the former magistrates have made many burgesses of gentlemen in the countrey to serve a turne. To secure this election it is necessary that there be a new charter which they are inclined to. They propose to choose Henry Bridges and William Coward, both right.

Taunton.—Is a Corporation; the election is popular and consists of about 700. A new charter is requisite, for till then ye inhabitants are awed by the country gentlemen who are their magistrates. A *Quo Warranto* is sent, on which their charter will be deliverd. The greatest part of the towne are dissenters, & doe propose to choose John Trenchard and Edward Clarke, both right; but if your Matie be not satisfied in Mr Trenchard, they will choose William Clarke, or who your Mat^{ie} will name, or Mr Brent recommend.

Bridgwater.—Is a Corporation; the election is popular to about 240. They doe propose to choose Sr John Bowden & Sr Hazwell Tent; the first is undoubtedly right, the other not doubted by the dissenters. It is requisite for Sr John Bowden to appear at the election, elce Sr Francis Warr, who is a very ill man, will be chosen. He industriously makes an intrest for itt.

Mynhead.—Is a Corporation; the election popular. The

towne belongs to Coll. Lutterell, of whom we can yett give not account. Who he proposes will be chosen here, except the sheriff can improve the interest of John Speak and Robert Sinderfin (who are both right), which he hath promised to doe.

Ilchester.—Is a Corporation; the election is popular; consists of about 140. A new charter is requesite in order wherunto a *Quo Warranto* is served, and the charter had bin delivered had nott Sr Edward Phillips advised the contrary. They will choose Edward Strode, the sheriff, if your Matie will permitt itt, and John Speke, both right men, and who will have interest to carry itt, especially when theres a new charter.

Milborne Port.—Is a Corporation; the election is popular. Mr Henry Bull and Mr John Hunt, two verry ill men, have made interest to be chosen on promise that they will oppose the takeing away of the test. A *Quo Warranto* is requesite, on which it's supposed they will rather consent (then loose their charter) to choose Sr Charles Cartwright and William Strode, who are both right men.

In Sept. 1688 the 'agents in the country' sent up a further report of the progress they had made.

The dissenters were reported trim to their resolutions and not shaken by any endeavours used to the contrary. The books that have been disperst have had a very good effect, though great endeavours have been made by the Church party to disswade people from reading them.

The great inconvenience attending this affair is the suggestions propagated by Churchmen, and others disaffected residing about London.

However, we have no reason to doubt but that there will be an election of members that will readily concur.

Then follows an account, so far as could be learned from the electors, of ' who they intend to choose,' and their respective inclinations.

Somerset.—They have not yet pitched upon who they will elect. The sheriff and the dissenters there will do their utmost to secure a good election.

Bath.—They resolve to choose Sr William Basset and Mr Oliver Nicholls.

Taunton.—Will choose John Trenchard & Edward Clerke. Sr Humphrey Mackworth is a stranger and hath no interest there: and if they should endeavour his election they might hazard the whole. For Sr Wm Portman and Mr Sandford, their last members, are making a party in that towne, but will faile if the two first stand.

Bridgwater.—Will choose Sr Haswell Tynt and Sr John Bawden if he appears upon the spott; otherwise Mr George Musgrave will be chosen.

Sr Francis Warr, a violent Churchman, labours his owne election.

Minehead.—The sheriff hath undertaken the care of this place, and to propose right men, which they could not fix upon when our friends were upon the spott.

Ilchester.—Will elect John Speake & William Strode, if neither of them be elected in the county; if they be, another fitt man will be pitched upon.

Sr Edwd Philips attempts to make an interest to oppose this election.

Milborn Port.—Sr Charles Carteret will be elected, and he hath interest to influence the election of another fitt person. He is to be spoke with about it. William Lacy Esq. is proposed as fitt.

Mr Hunt and Mr Bull, their two last members, endeavour to be elected, but supposed will be fruitless.

In the first revision of Deputy Lieutenants in December, 1685, the following Somerset names were submitted to the king:

Lord Fitzharding
Francis Paulett, Esq.

Sir William Bassett.
William Lucy, Esq.

New Ones.

Sir Hugh Tynte.
Sir Thos Bridges.
Edward Strode, Esqr.
Edward Clarke, Esqr.
Robert Syderfin, Esqr.

Baldwin Mallett, Esqr.
Warwick Bampfield, Esqr.
John Anthill, Esqr.
Charles Steyning, Esqr.

Justices of the Peace.

William Clarke, Esqr.
Henry Walrond, Esqr.
Richard Crosse, Esqr.
Peter Reynon, Esqr.

Thos Littleton, Esqr.
George Hussey, Esqr.
John Brent, Esqr.
Robert Brent, Esqr.

New Ones.

John Harrington, Esqr.
John Champney, Esqr.
Sr Charles Carteret, Esqr.
William Coward, Esqr.

William Strode, Esqr.
George Musgrave, Esqr.
John Speke, Esqr.
Abraham Atkins, Esqr.

In the second revision, February, 1688, the list included:

Lord Viscount Fitzharding.
Sir William Bassett.
William Lucy, Esqr.
Sir Hugh Tynt.
Sir Thomas Bridges.
Edward Strode, Esqr.

Edward Clarke, Esqr.
Robert Synderfin, Esqr.
Thomas Moore, Esqr.
Warwick Bampfeild, Esqr.
Francis Ancketill, Esqr.
John Harrington, Esqr.

Justices of the Peace.

William Clarke, Esqr.
Henry Walrond, Esqr.
Richard Cross, Esqr.
Peter Reynon, Esqr.
Thomas Littleton, Esqr.
William Strode, Esqr.
George Musgrave, Esqr.
John Speak, Esqr.
Abraham Atkins, Esqr.
Thomas Baynard, Esqr.
Thomas Strode, Esqr.
Henry Gould, Esqr.
George Longe, Esqr.
William How, Esqr.
Samuel Cabell, Esqr.
Gore, Esqr.
Henry Rolls, Esqr.
Harry Bridges, Esqr.

George Hussey, Esqr.
Robert Brent, Esqr.
John Champney, Esqr.
Sir Charles Carterett.
William Coward, Esqr.
Richard Cross, Esqr.
James Webb, Esqr
Edward Hobbs, Esqr.
Henry Henley.
Henry Longe.
Francis Vaughan.
Richard Jones.
Thomas Muttlebury.
Andrew Cross.
Henry Mompesson.
John Burland.
Thomas Hawker.
~~Richard Glanvill~~.

The last name is erased as here marked.

Plots against the king and his proceedings were by now constantly reported; but the papers preserved relating to this time are so few that detailed information is not available. Notwithstanding a full knowledge of such feelings, the king's intentions and determination did not alter. Rather it would seem that the reports of his emissaries gave him and his advisers more confidence, as on April 7, 1688, just as a year had elapsed, the ' declaration ' was issued for the second time, with the additional announcement that: ' Our conduct ought to have persuaded the world that we are firm in our resolutions, but that easie people may not be abused by crafty wicked men, we declare our intentions are not changed.' This was ordered to be read in all churches May 20 and 27. On this matter seven bishops refused obedience, one of them Bishop Ken of Bath and Wells, the result being the well-known historic event, their trial and acquittal.

Amongst the few State Papers preserved there is the information of one Elias Bragg, who was to be found at the sign of the Ship in Bridgwater, as to a plot of which he had learned.

Bragg had gone to Bristol to be ' lett blood for a complaint of dizziness,' and there in conversation said that he had just returned from Holland, and had brought over a hundred and fifty letters for London, and fifty for Bristol; further, that forty thousand men would soon be landed in Cornwall, under the name of Irish, and forty thousand more at Plymouth. Monmouth would be in command.'[1] He gave the names of those implicated in Somerset as being Esq. Henley; Sir Thos Bridges and his son: Mr Green of Redland; Sir John Rolls of Cannington; Sir John Smith; Esq. Jones of Hinton Bluett; and Esq. Jones of Clutton. Some of these 'had then been for some days at Downside, at Esq. Strode's the head sheriff of Somerset and Esq. Strode's was the place of meeting for the persons deepest concerned.' Had this story been true this last paragraph would have added another curious note to the

[1] Monmouth was believed to be still alive.

Strode history. The informer who had received this story, having unburdened himself, was at once committed to gaol for misprision of treason in suffering Bragg to escape, but was liberated on the latter being taken by the Mayor of Bridgewater. Elias Bragg alias Clarke, of Curry Rivel, was brought up for examination at Ilchester on April 25. It appeared that he had been one of Monmouth's men at Taunton, and after the failure was sent to Bridewell there. His story was that, about a fortnight before Michaelmas, as he was travelling with the carrier to Exeter, he asked to be directed to any gentleman wanting a servant, he having lived in that capacity with Madam Jennings of Curry Rivel. Going to a house at Otterton for this purpose, he there found a 'Conventicle Meeting,' which he seems to have joined, and so pretended to have learned what was in progress—namely, that men would be landed in Wales, and others at Minehead and Porlock. There were present, he said, Madame Pyne and two of her sons, one having been a captain in the late rebellion; Mr. Prideaux of Ford, Mr. Henley of Leigh, Mr. Savage of Taunton, who was one of Monmouth's captains, and Captain Speak, who had served in the late rebellion. Mr. Speak was in the hall. Bragg stated that he agreed to carry letters and to go to Bristol to the Marsh to see what cannon lay there, that Monmouth's men might take them to Minehead and Porlock; but, getting 'troubled in his mind,' he discovered the plot. The matter caused some excitement. Mr. Henry Bridges, reporting the meeting to examine him, says that eighteen justices appeared, 'a greater appearance seldom known, and for conduct and despatch of business free from the usual clashing and violence.' He had expected to find the prisoner a 'man of periwig, cravat, and address such as Bedloe;' but he saw 'a meer worm who pretended to make mumping worth thirty shillings per diem, besides meat and drink,' by carrying about these tales. He was vexed at so much trouble about so frivolous a trifle, void of all credit.

On the meeting of the justices Lord Fitzharding wrote a letter recommending them to elect Mr. Clerk of Sandeford as chairman. As Mr. Clerk had sold all he had in Somerset, and at the time lived chiefly in Wilts, this, it was thought, 'savoured more of imposition' upon the meeting than any 'intention of good service.' The request was consequently refused, and Mr. Coward, Recorder of Wells, was importuned to take the chair. After a modest refusal he acceded, and 'gave a charge to the grand jury second to none but Cicero himself.' During this meeting a *Quo Warranto* was issued against the charter of Ilchester, and after some 'persuasion' the bailiff and burgesses, twelve in number, resolved to deliver it, the bailiff undertaking to carry it to London the next week.

What was going on in another way may be gathered from a letter of the time, dated Wells, May 19, concerning the 'great mischief and uncertainty proceeding from the county post houses.' The king's affairs, said the writer, 'might be treated with more secresy than I fear they are, through the malice of prying people.' In particular was mentioned a complaint from Yeovil, 'the staple commodity whereof is gloving,' where the complainant, who 'paid £5 or £6 a year postage,' stated that the postmaster, through ill will towards him, 'stifled' his letters to his great damage. Another letter 'of great consequence' was 'stifled' at Bruton. If, says the writer, the villainy of other counties equals this, no account of any consequence can be transmitted without passing the 'pykes' of these men.

The discontent having now worked up an organised opposition, some direct overtures were made to the Prince of Orange, who, by his marriage to the king's daughter Mary, was next heir to the throne. The prince hesitated, as was but natural, inasmuch as by waiting, should he survive the king, he must succeed. But it happened that another cause of discontent arose when in June the queen was announced to have given birth to a son—a child which nearly every one considered supposititious—a birth hardly any one believed to be other than an imposition. As by this event the Prince of Orange entirely lost all chance of succession, he was at last induced to action. By September the prince's intentions were known, so that the king, thoroughly alarmed, was obliged to take defensive measures. The first movement was on September 24, when he signified that he would call a Parliament in November, coupling with this promise the announcement that it was his 'royal purpose by so doing to endeavour a legal establishment of liberty of conscience,' the inference here being an acknowledgment that the then position was illegal. Matters now moved apace; the position seems to have been suddenly realised; a thorough fear seems to have been established.

On September 26, only two days later, the removed deputy-lieutenants were restored.

On the 28th came out a proclamation declaring that an armed force intended an invasion from Holland, 'promoted, as we understand, by some of our subjects, wicked, restless spirits.'

On October 2 a general pardon was issued, among the exceptions being Laurence Braddon.

On October 11 a form of prayer was issued, to be used

during this time of public apprehension. Herein it was prayed for the king: 'Inspire him with wisdom and justice. Give all his subjects grace always to bear faith and true allegiance.'

On October 17 corporations were restored.

On November 5 came news from Brixham that a fleet with the Prince of Orange had arrived, and that the men were landing.

On November 6 a proclamation declared the invasion 'only to be thought of with horror, as unchristian and unnatural in one so nearly related, especially as he calls in question the legitimacy of our son.'

Meanwhile the king sent troops to Salisbury, and went there himself to join them. The prince, commencing his march, advanced towards Exeter; the movement being made during some hours of the night, in darkness and rain, proved a hard and rough trial for his men. There was at first, too, but little appearance of support from the district, as all were afraid 'they would be served as the Duke of Monmouth's men were served.' Camping at last this night without shelter in a stubble field, 'verily the water ran over and under them, and their heads, backs and arms sunk into the red clay;' yet, being weary, they 'slept very sweetly in their pee or campaign coats.'[1]

By November 9 the prince had arrived at Exeter, and here the report reached him that the king had resolved to await and fight him near Salisbury. At Exeter the Somerset gentry 'came in briskly,' being well provided with all things useful in abundance, especially with the sinews of war. With those

[1] *Diary of the March of the Prince of Orange.*

who came were Sir Francis Warre, Sir William Portman, Col. Luttrell and his brother, Major Palmer, Mr. Speke, Sir Edward Seymour, Mr. Thomas Seymour, Col. Bampfield, Col. Thomas Wyndham and his son, Mr. Stawell, Mr. Mallet, and Capt. Braddon.[1] On November 15 they presented an address as follows:—

We, whose names are hereunto subscribed, who have now joyned with the Prince of Orange for the defence of the Protestant religion, and for maintaining the ancient Government and the laws and liberties of England, Scotland and Ireland, do engage to Almighty God, to his Highness the Prince of Orange, and to one another, to stick firm to the cause and to one another in the defence of it, and never to depart from it until our religion, our laws and liberties are so far secured to us in a free Parliament, that we shall be no more in danger of falling under popery and slavery. And whereas we are engaged in this common cause under the protection of the Prince of Orange, by which means his person may be exposed to dangers, and to the desperate cursed attempts of papists and other bloody men:—We do therefore solemnly engage to God and to one another, that if any such attempts are made upon him, we will pursue not only those who make them, but all their adherents and all that we find in arms against us with the utmost severity of a just revenge to their ruin and destruction, and that the execution of such attempts (which God of his mercy forbid) shall not divert us from prosecuting this cause, which we now undertake, but that it shall engage us to carry it on with all the rigour that so barbarous a practice shall deserve against all persons whatsoever, the king's sacred person only excepted.

[1] *Hist. MSS. Seventh Report.*

Signed by:—

Fitz Harding.	Ha Roynon.
Stawell.	
J⁰ Portman.	J. Doddington.
John Smythe.	John Hody.
	Wᴹ Westley.
George Horner.	John Sanford.
Edwᴅ Beazeley.	W. Roynon.
	Geo Wickeam.
T. A. Gorges.	W Wickeam.
Tʜ Mompesson.	
Hugh Hellier.	J. Pryse.
John Pigott.	Thoˢ Poole.
Edwᴅ Baker.	H. Welsted.
Henry Mompesson.	Thomas Jackson.
J. Henry Gould.	John Watts.
Henry Walrond.	Jer Newcombe.
John Bailey.	David Williams.
Joseph Godwyn.	N. Palmer.
John Sandys.	Ed Bowyer.
George Musgrave.	
Luke Morgan.	Thoˢ Willie.
War Bampfield.	John
Geo Long.	
Richᴅ Cox.	John Burdon.
James Webb.	Hobbes.
Tho Sambourne.	John Day.

The names omitted are illegible.[1]

On Nov. 15 the prince made them the following speech in reply:—

[1] MSS. Sir A. Hood.

Tho we know not all your persons, yet we have a catalogue of your names, and remember the character of your worth and interest in the county. You see we are come according to your invitation and our promise. Our duty to God obliges us to protect the Protestant religion; and our love to mankind, your liberties and properties. We expected you that dwelt so near the place of our landing would have joined us sooner, not that it is now too late, nor that we want your military assistance so much as your countenance and presence, to justify our declared pretensions, rather than accomplish our good and gracious designs. Tho we have both a good fleet, and a good army, to render these kingdoms happy, by rescuing all Protestants from popery, slavery, and arbitrary power; by restoring them in their rights and properties established by law, and by promoting peace and trade, which is the soul of Government, and the very life-blood of a nation; yet we rely more on the goodness of God and the justice of our cause, than on any human force and power whatever. Yet since God is pleased we shall make use of human means, and not expect miracles, for our preservation and happiness, let us not neglect making use of this gracious opportunity, but with prudence and courage put in execution our so honourable purposes. Therefore, gentlemen, friends, and fellow-Protestants, we bid you and all your followers most heartily welcome to our court and camp. Let the whole world now judge, if our pretentions are not just, generous, sincere, and above price, since we might have even a bridge of gold to return back. But it is our principle and resolution, rather to die in a good cause, than live in a bad one, well knowing that virtue and true honour is its own reward, and the happiness of mankind our great and only design.[1]

[1] Fourth Collection of Papers, etc.

Refreshed by the stay at Exeter, one man afterwards being as good as two before, the force advanced in three divisions, each division being a day or so behind the other. The prince accompanied the middle or second division; the people, everywhere anxious to see him, followed him wherever he passed. The first division marched first to St. Mary Ottery; the next day the second division marched to the same place, the first then advancing to Axminster. Then the third division advanced to Ottery, the second to Axminster and Lyme, and the first to Beaminster and Crookhorn. So, after the third division had left Exeter, the whole force moved simultaneously. Oxen were used for the artillery, horses for the ammunition. The first line moving to Sherborne, the prince with the second 'rode to Crookhorn with a noble attendance,' the people flocking in great numbers to see him. At Crookhorn he remained Sunday, November 25. Here, besides many gentlemen of the West, a regiment of royal infantry and the officers of a dragoon regiment joined him.[1] The first line now marched to Wincanton; the second following to Sherborne, whither went also the prince and lodged at the castle, being thus advanced directly upon the king's troops.

Here Dr. Finch, Warden of All Souls College, Oxford, came to the prince from the heads of other colleges, with the assurance that they would declare for him if he came there, and that their plate should be at his service.

From Sherborne was issued a celebrated document known as the Prince's Third Declaration.[2]

The prince's first declaration was dated October 10, to which an additional one was added, dated October 24. In the first

[1] *Hist. MSS. Seventh Report.* [2] Burnet, *Hist. of Own Time.*

was sketched the conduct of the evil counsellors about the king; the various complaints of the country; and the dismal effect of the assumption of arbitrary power. And it adds, to crown all, there were the great and violent presumptions regarding the birth of a son. During the queen's pretended bigness, and in the manner in which the birth was managed, there were so many just and visible grounds of suspicion that not only himself, but all good subjects vehemently suspected that the pretended child was not born of the queen. And since 'our dearest consort and our selfs have so great an interest in this matter, and a right to the succession, we cannot excuse ourselves from espousing the interests of the English people, and contributing to maintain the Protestant religion, the laws and liberties of the three kingdoms.'

The third declaration, having every appearance of being genuine, was dated Sherborne Castle, November 28. Its effect was immediate and widespread, as its wording so exactly caught the feeling and wishes of the time. It declared the prince's fervent zeal for the Protestant religion, his resolution to rescue the country from slavery and popery, and that he was resolved to call a free Parliament forthwith. It further promised that no injury should be done to any one; not even to a papist except when found in arms; then he should be treated as a robber and bandit, and 'intirely delivered up to the discretion of the souldiers.'

This momentous document was afterwards found to be unauthorised, and for a long time its authorship remained unacknowledged. Sir Hugh Speke eventually claimed it as his: 'I wrote it first, and when it was perfected to my liking, I then sealed it up in a sheet of paper and left it with a person in London that I could trust, and charged him to keep the paper till he heard from me out of the west by letter after I was got to the Prince of Orange, and then to dispose of it as I should direct.' Having informed himself of the exact route and plan of marching from Exeter, Sir Hugh wrote to London accordingly, ordering the insertion of the words 'Given under our hand at Sherborne,' and that the manuscript should be put under a certain bookseller's door, the said bookseller receiving an order to print.[1]

Be the authorship where it may, this document practically in its effect secured all for the prince.

It being reported that some of the prince's party had advanced into Somerset as far as Bruton, thither went Col. Sarsfield from Salisbury with some royal troopers. The colonel, however, missed his intention, as, on his arrival at Bruton, the others had marched to Wincanton, whither he followed on November 20. Lieutenant Campbell at Wincanton, in command of about twenty-five men, hearing of Sarsfield's approach, resolved to fight him. First he posted the majority of his men in a small enclosure at the 'east end of the town on the left side,' a good hedge being between them and the road by which their enemy must come. Just opposite this spot, in a little garden also covered by a thick hedge, he placed six men, and then, with four or five others, he took the road, determined to be cautious and not to fire too hastily, as there was the possibility that Sarsfield's men would desert and join him. Presently Sarsfield and his men were seen approaching. Waiting until they were quite near, Campbell then challenged with : 'Stand ! stand ! for whom are ye ?' To this the other replied, 'I am for King James : who art thou for ?' Campbell answered, 'For the Prince of Orange.' 'God damn me !' returned the other, 'I'll Prince thee.' Hearing this, Campbell ordered his men to fire, and, himself going up to this 'popish

[1] Speke, H. *Some Memoirs of Remarkable Passages*, 1709.

officer,' shot him in at the mouth and through the brains; so he dropped down dead. Firing now commenced on both sides; but the royalists, a hundred and fifty strong—the *Gazette* says a hundred and twenty, seventy horse, and fifty dragoons—got into the field, some through a dead hedge, some at the lower corner, others by a little gate said to have been opened by a countryman who was looking on; and so they quickly surrounded their opponents, who could do nothing more than fire as fast as possible. Defending themselves thus stubbornly, they were joined by their companions from the other side of the road, but at last were overpowered by numbers. The wounded, some of them shot in five or six places, being offered quarter for their bravery, 'would not accept it from the hands of papists,' but chose rather to die. Every man would have been killed had not a miller riding into the town proclaimed to the townspeople, who in alarm and terror had thronged into the streets, that a strong party of Orange horsemen was just on entering on the other side. The miller further called out to the king's men, 'Away! away for your lives! save yourselves! the enemies are at hand!' On hearing this and seeing the great confusion in the streets, the troopers judged it was true and galloped away.

The result of all this was that, on the Orange side, Lieutenant Campbell and eight or nine others were killed, and six prisoners were taken, of whom, however, three got away. Of the king's side four were reported killed and two wounded. If the two wounded died, the general account may be considered correct, as in the end fifteen dead were tumbled into one grave. This narrative was taken from Mr. Bulgin the minister; and from Cornet Webb of the king's force as he lay wounded, shot through the back and reins.[1]

[1] *Diary of the March of the Prince of Orange.*

Besides this, the only episode in Somerset was the arrival of a party of Orangemen at Bridgwater, where they secured some twenty horses from the market people.

Although both the main forces had been very near each other, no general encounter happened, as the king at Salisbury, unable to depend on his men, finding them disloyal and deserting him, hastily left them and returned to Windsor and so to London. His camp then broke up in disorder, and many of the officers and soldiers joined the prince.

From Sherborne the prince, with now Prince George of Denmark and many others who had left the king, marched to Wincanton. When leaving here, a royal trumpeter arrived asking a pass for messengers to treat.[1] So the prince, Sir Wm. Portman being with him, advanced by Mere to Salisbury. From here the force passed across the plain by Stonehenge, where a halt was made to view the novel sight, considered to be a monument erected to commemorate some notable victory. All then moved on to Collingbourn Kingston, then to Hungerford, where the prince lay at Littlecot, and then to Windsor.

Besides the fight at Wincanton there was but one other skirmish throughout this memorable march, this being an encounter between the English and Irish at Reading. Of all the folly committed by James, the bringing over Irish soldiers, papists too, to aid him, was perhaps the greatest. Looked upon at the time as little better than savages, the feeling of shame was widespread, with terror superadded at the fear of the murders and outrages always known to accompany the presence of these men.

By some means, still unknown by whom, although the merit of it has been claimed by a Speke, a rumour was spread that some Irish were advancing on various places. A letter

[1] *Hist. MSS. Seventh Report.*

from Yeovil, dated December 19, 1688,[1] records that about three in the morning the whole town was alarmed by a report that some thousands of Irish were marching westward, having burned Portsmouth, Lymington, and Basingstoke. This report revived the remembrance that during the civil war some Irish had landed on the Somerset coast, and committed many atrocities. The country round as far as Taunton rose at once in arms. All sorts of weapons were seized. Some had swords, some muskets, some clubs, several thousands both horse and foot being thus ready. The report, however, proved to be a false alarm, to the no small joy of everybody.

The next event was the escape and flight of the king. Consequent on this, on December 11, instead of a royal proclamation, there came out a declaration of the Lords spiritual and temporal announcing that the king had fled. Next it was ordered that a deputation should wait on the prince, and that all papists should be disarmed, and all jesuits and priests secured.

On December 22, when the nobility declared in favour of the prince and against the late king's proceedings, 'as rendering the laws a nose of wax,' the streets were thronged with people all rejoicing at being redeemed from 'popery and slavery.' Thus the revolution was complete. How the Somerset men sang we learn from a ballad entitled:—' The Courageous Soldiers of the West, or, The undaunted Countrymens Resolution in taking up arms in defence of King William and Queen Mary, together with the Protestant Religion.' Tune is: 'Lilli Borlero.'[2] Woodcut: soldiers marching.

[1] *London Mercury.*   [2] *Bagford Ballads.*

Now to maintain the Protestant cause,
   All the whole West does loyally stand,
For our lives, religion and laws,
   Roman shall never reign in this land.
Stout lads brisk and airy, for William and Mary,
They'll valiantly fight their rights to maintain.

Bridgewater boys I needs must commend,
   Freely they to the wars did repair,
Parents and wife, nay, every friend,
   They recommend to Heaven's great care;
Life and fortune freely venter,
Nothing alive true courage can stain.
Stout lads brisk and airy, for William and Mary,
They'll valiantly fight their rights to maintain.

As for the town of brave Taunton-dean,
   Their loyalty shall ne'er be forgot,
For our most gracious king and his queen,
   They will engage with thundering shot.
Noble true souls came flocking amain.
Stout lads brisk and airy, for William and Mary,
They'll valiantly fight their rights to maintain.

A most important factor, as already mentioned, in producing the result here sketched was the birth of the P. P., as he was called (Pretended Prince), an event to which a few observations may be devoted.

Of the many powers attributed to the Bath waters, one, now transferred to others farther away, was that of removing barrenness in women—a belief traced as existing from an early time. It may be said that this belief contributed much to give a special character to the place. So much was this power of the waters assumed that, when a childless woman arrived at Bath, it was usual to make the remark, 'She comes for the common cause.'

Acting on this custom, the childless queen having determined to go to the Bath, arrived there from Windsor on August 18, 1687, joining the king, who had arrived from Portsmouth about an hour before her. The queen stayed at Dr. Peirce's at the Abbey House, where she was to be prepared, as it was called. Dr. Peirce had written on the effects of these waters in curing palsy and barrenness, and this being published in the 'Philosophical Transactions' for 1685 was thus stamped with authority.

The example cited was that of a gentlewoman of Wells, aged about 30 or 32, who had been married ten or twelve years, without being with child. Being seized with palsy in the left side, she was brought to Bath, where she remained some time. After the 'usual preparations and some internal means,' she recovered the use of her hand, leg, and tongue, and not only so, but 'in a few weeks after she returned to her husband, conceived with child, and had at about a year and half distance between them five children.'

Other medicos record similar cases.

The king stayed a few days at Bath, and then went northwards alone. Returning to Bath on September 6, he again remained a few days, and finally returned to Windsor alone.

The queen stayed on until October 6, when she also returned to Windsor.

Soon after her return it began to be reported that she was with child, and further that she had immediately conceived on being with the king on the very day of her arrival from Bath. The future event was therefore calculated as from this October 6. It was also circulated that at the very moment of this conception, the queen's mother was making a vow to the Lady of Loretto, praying that her daughter might conceive and have a son, the offering made being a flaming heart and two golden angels worth 60,000*l*.

Too evidently intending to keep up this belief regarding the Bath waters, the king later urged the Princess Anne of Denmark, who had miscarried, to go to the Bath for her general health. To this she assented, and went there towards the end of May, 1688. She was thus thought to be out of the queen's way, her interest in the succession being too near to allow her to join in any deception.

Preparations had been made and were making for the queen's delivery, all to be ready by the end of June; but no sooner was Anne gone than suddenly the queen changed the reckoning and declared the start must be made a month earlier, or from the time the king returned to her at Bath, viz., September 6. This being reported to the princess at Bath, she was urged to return at once. The queen, learning this on Wednesday, ordered her lodgings at St. James's to be ready by Saturday for her lying-in. Being told that this could not be done, she became enraged and sent an order that the bed must be ready, and 'let the worst come to the worst she would lye in on Saturday though only blankets were nailed about the bed.'[1] Accordingly, on June 10, instead of in July, no one but Italian ladies being present, the English and Protestants being away or at church, the birth was said to have occurred.

Outside it was quickly perceived that the time did not agree with the early announcement, and the child was at once set down to be an imposition. The pamphleteers and gossips had their chance, and many and curious are the issues of this time. A council was held on October 22 to consider these accusations, and to gather evidence of the birth, and the fatal resolution was then taken to publish a defence against all this 'false news and slander, of late more bold an

[1] *Hist. MSS. Ninth Report*, p. 469A.

licentious than formerly.' Counter publications were at once issued, and the 'defence' mercilessly pulled to pieces.

On the announcement of the birth some addresses of course came up. Very few they were, but of them four are from Somerset, two of these being from Bath, all as before being printed in the *London Gazette*. First, on July 19, 1688, came out:

The Humble Address of the Clothiers of the Counties of Devon and Somerset.

MAY IT PLEASE YOUR MAJESTY.

We cannot but in a due sense of your Majesties great goodness to us, tender our most humble and hearty thanks for your gracious hearing our miserable complaint of the exportation of wooll, and of your Majesties speedy as well as effectual redress thereof, in issuing out your commission for that purpose, by which your Majesty hath preserved and put a new life to trade, which next to the great and glorious design of liberty of conscience, is undoubtedly the best support of the wealth and grandeur of a nation, and therefore we can now return with joy to our respective habitations.

And as it hath pleased God, to our great joy, to bless your Majesty with a royal prince to sway the scepter of these kingdoms after your Majesty: so we heartily pray God there may never want of your princely posterity to sit on the throne of your Majesty; and that he may in due time inherit your princely virtues, as well as the just dominion over all your kingdoms.

On July 26 was printed:—

The Humble and Unanimous Congratulation of his Majesties Justices of the Peace for the County of Somerset, at their

General Quarter Sessions held at Bridgwater the Tenth Day of July in the Fourth Year of his Majesties Reign, Anno Dom. 1688. Subscribed likewise by several other gentlemen then and there present.

MOST GRACIOUS SOVEREIGN,

Although we have with all sincerity made our respective acknowledgments to Almighty God for the great blessing He hath vouchsafed this nation, by making your Majesty the parent of a most hopeful and illustrious prince, and have given as great and ample demonstrations of our joy for the same in our several stations as we were capable, yet nevertheless we do not think our selves acquitted of our duty without an humble congratulation with your Majesty and your royal consort upon this happy occasion, and assuring your Majesty, that whenever the overruling power (by which kings reign) shall resume that crown you now so justly wear, we will bear all faith and true allegiance to this illustrious prince; but that the commencement thereof may be late, are, and shall always be, the prayers of,

Your Majesties most faithful and most
Obedient Subjects.

The first from Bath, dated June 25, and printed July 30, was :—

To the King's most Excellent Majesty,

The hearty congratulation of the Mayor, Aldermen, and Common Council, of your Majesty's City of Bath.

DREAD SOVEREIGN!

No sooner did the happy news of a prince being born reach our ears, but we thought it our duty to congratulate your Majesty for so great a blessing : and knowing it is un-

THROUGH THE COUNTY OF SOMERSET 71

just to be silent on this occasion, we do therefore offer up our thanks to the great Jehovah, for sending an heir to your Majesty and your kingdoms from your royal loyns; which is that alone can confirm our present happiness under your government, and give us a comfortable prospect of the continuance of it. And we, as far as in us lies, shall, in our proper station, contribute to the assisting your Majesty in your pious intentions, in setling these your kingdoms in peace and tranquility, whensoever your most sacred Majesty shall in your princely wisdom think fit to require it of us. And we heartily implore the Almighty to send your Majesty and us more such royal pledges by your gracious consort; and bless your Majesty with long life to see our young prince, by your Majesty's tender care, fitted to govern all his people. These are the prayers of us, your Majesty's most dutiful and obedient subjects. In testimony whereof we have hereunto affixed our common seal this 25th day of June, in the fourth year of your Majesty's reign.

This was followed on August 6 by another:—

To the King's most Excellent Majesty,

The Humble Gratulatory Address of several Members of the Corporation, and other Freemen and Inhabitants of your ancient City of Bath.

MAY IT PLEASE YOUR MAJESTY,

No sooner did the happy news of the prince's birth reach our ears, but we of this place thought it our duty, in a more especial manner, to be early in the return of our praises to the Almighty, for so great a blessing upon us and your three kingdoms, and in congratulating your Majesty and your royal consort of being the joyful parents of so goodly a son; a gift which the whole nation ought to esteem as the reward of Heaven, upon that continued series of goodness and indulgence which your Majesty hath ever since the beginning of your most auspicious reign extended to your subjects, particularly that of your compassionate declaration for liberty of conscience; whereby as you are pleased to suspend the execution of all penal laws in matters of religion, and the requiring of any oaths or tests from any; so do we, upon our allegiance to you our sovereign, promise and engage, that whensoever your Majesty shall think fit to call a Parliament, such of us as shall have a power of electing, will chuse none to serve therein, but who shall give us a full assurance, that they will endeavour the total abrogation of them.

And that your Majesty may have the ready concurrence of both your houses in these gracious intentions; and enjoy the comfort and satisfaction of seeing the fruits and consequences thereof, by a long and prosperous reign in peace and plenty, (having survived the murmurings and discontents of a malevolent party) the prince your son arrived to maturity of years and understanding; and a numerous offspring from your royal loyns, which may perpetuate your name and memory, and even baffle mortality itself, shall be the constant prayer of,
  Dread Sovereign,
    Your Majesties ever dutiful and loyal Subjects.

Yet with all this apparent subserviency Bath was as thankful as any place when the king was gone, and the next year had her rejoicings with the rest when the new king was crowned. One broadside poem on this subject is entitled:

'The Loyalty and Glory of the City of Bath : being a True and Perfect Relation of the Wonderful Ceremony and Transactions that were lately performed there.'

Another is: 'News from Bath: being a true and perfect Relation of the great and splendid Procession and joyful Transactions there, on the 11th day of April; being the Coronation-day of their most sacred Majesties William and Mary, King and Queen of England, Scotland, France and Ireland.'

In this it is told that a great number of the best quality joined in the festivities in testimony of their joy for the happy deliverance from popery and slavery. In the procession of the day, first came a hundred young men in holland shirts richly adorned and carrying naked swords in their hands as a protection to the succeeding train of two hundred virgins girt with 'bagonets' and clad in rich attire, with crowns on their heads and sceptres in their hands. They carried also two flags : on one, ' God save King William and Queen Mary; let their enemies perish.' And on the other, ' This is a joyful day.' Next, carrying a truncheon gilt, came an 'Amazon dame' clad in a velvet escalloped vesture covered with gold lace, a golden sash on her waist, and on her head a light peruke crowned with a plume of crimson feathers. Following her were twenty-four others of her sex, dressed in like manner, but carrying darts and javelins in their hands, their 'right paps concealed' so as to appear cut off. Next came thirty young gentlewomen each carrying a bow and arrow and having a scarf on her shoulder, a laurel crown on her head, and on her breast the motto, 'Rather than lose the day we'll fight.' Then came the militia with drums and colours, accompanied by 'acclamations of unforced joy' exceeding anything ever seen. After marching round the city twice, they entered the Guildhall, where a 'sumptuous banquet' was ready—not touched, however, until by 'permission of the Amazons.' Dancing was kept up all night, the songs being

> In praise of him who came with Heaven's high hand
> To drive Rome's priests (those vipers) from our land.
> Those locusts that to Lucifer bespoke us,
> Whose mock religion is a hocus pocus.

A memorial cross was erected by the Earl of Melfort in the Cross Bath to commemorate, as the inscription told, the great power of the waters which had given an heir to three kingdoms: an unfortunate commemoration, for it may well be said that this embryo of the Bath Waters cost James II. his crown.

INDEX

Ancketill, F., 51.
Andrewes, R., 46.
Anne, of Denmark, 15.
Anthill, J., 31, 50.
Ashford, J., 29.
Atkins, A., 50, 51.
Axbridge, 13.
Axminster, 60.

Baber, E., 16.
Bailey, J., 58.
Baker, E., 58.
—— R., 26.
Balche, R., 27.
Bamfeild, W., 31, 50, 51, 58.
Bampfield, Col., 57.
Barrington, 44.
Basset, Sir W., 28, 31, 47, 49, 50, 51.
Bath, 10, 19, 20, 22, 30, 31, 38, 47, 49, 66, 67, 70, 71, 72, 73, 74.
Bathurst, Dr., 30.
Bawden, Sir J., 32, 47, 49.
Bayley, J., 30, 34.
Baynard, T., 51.
Beaminster, 60.
Beazeley, E., 58.

Berkeley, E., 30.
Bicknell, W., 27.
Blathwayt, W., 26.
Blewet, J., 30.
Bowyer, E., 58.
Braddon, Capt., 57.
—— L., 55.
Bragg, E., 52, 53.
Brent, J., 30, 50.
—— R., 30, 50, 51.
Bridges, H., 30, 32, 47, 51, 53.
—— Sir T., 30, 32, 47, 50, 51, 52.
Bridgwater, 3, 11, 16, 26, 27, 30, 32, 47, 49, 52, 53, 64, 70.
Bristol, 52.
Brixham, 56.
Bruton, 22, 33, 36, 37, 54, 62.
Bulgin, Mr., 63.
Bull, H., 29, 32, 34, 48, 50.
Burdon, J., 58.
Burland, J., 51.

Cabell, S., 51.
Cade, J., 30.
Campbell, Lieut., 62, 63.

Cannington, 52.
Carteret, Sir C., 30, 32, 49, 50, 51.
Cartwright, Sir C., 48.
Champneys, J., 50, 51.
Chard, 23, 24.
Charles II., King, 14.
Cheek, E., 37.
Chipsley, 31.
Clark, G. 30.
—— W., 29, 47, 50, 51.
Clarke, E., 31, 32, 47 49, 50.
Clerk, Mr., 54.
Clothiers, 69.
Clutton, 52.
Collingbourn Kingston, 64.
Conventicle Meeting, 53.
Corporations restored, 56.
Coward, W., 31, 32, 47, 50, 51, 54.
Cox, R., 58.
Criddle, W., 26.
Cromwell, R., 25.
Crookhorn, 60.
Cross, A., 51.
—— R., 29, 50, 51.
Curry, J., 26.
Curry Rivel, 53.

INDEX

Daw, R., 36, 43.
Day, J., 58.
Declaration of Toleration, 15.
Deputy-Lieutenants, 50, 51.
Dining customs, 37.
Doddington, J., 58.
Downside (Shepton), 45, 52.

Epicureans, 25.
Exeter, 56, 60.

Fagell's pamphlet, 46.
Fitzharding, Lord, 28, 31, 35, 36, 37, 38, 41, 42, 50, 51, 54, 58.
Ford, 53.
Francklin, J., 27.
Frome, 22.

George, of Denmark, 15, 64.
Gilbert, J., 27.
Glanvill, R., 51.
Glastonbury, 31.
Glove trade, 54.
Godolphin, Lord, 40.
Godwyn, J., 58.
Gore, Esq., 51.
Gorges, E., 30.
—— T. A., 58.
Gould, H., 51.
—— J. H., 58.
Green, Mr., 52.
Greisley, F., 30.

Harrington, J., 30, 50, 51.
Hawker, T., 51.

Hellier, H., 58.
—— W., 29.
Henley, H., 51, 52, 53.
Hinton Bluett, 52.
Hoare, R., 27.
Hobbs, E., 51, 58.
Hody, J., 58.
Holt, Dr., 30.
Horner, G., 29, 58.
How, W., 51.
Hungerford, 64.
Hunt, J., 30, 32, 34, 35, 36, 41, 42, 48, 50.
Hussey, G., 30, 50, 51.

Ilchester, 32, 44, 48, 49, 53, 54.
Inscombe, 22.
Irish soldiers, 64; 65.

Jackson, T., 58.
James II., King, 14, 26, 64, 65, 74.
Jeffreys, Judge, 16.
Jennings, Madam, 53.
Jones, Esq. (Clutton), 52.
—— Esq. (Hinton Bluett), 52.
—— J., 45.
—— R., 51.

Ken, T. (Bishop), 52.

Lacye, W., 29, 50, 51.
Lantdon, J., 30.
Leigh, 53.
Littlecot, 64.
Littleton, T., 30, 50, 51.
Longe, G., 51, 58.
—— H., 51.
Lucy, see Lacey.

Lutterell, Col., 48, 57.
—— F., 29, 32.

Mackworth, Sir H., 49.
Malet, B., 31, 50.
—— Sir J., 3.
Mallet, Mr., 57.
Mary, of Orange, 15, 55.
Masy, W., 26.
Melfort, Earl of, 74.
Mere, 64.
Milborne Port, 22, 30, 32, 48, 49.
Minehead, 32, 47, 49, 53.
Ministers of East Somerset, 22.
—— West Somerset, 18.
Mompesson, H., 51, 58.
—— T., 58.
Monmouth, Duke of, 14, 15, 20, 39, 44, 45, 52, 53, 56.
Moore, T., 51.
Morgan, L., 58.
—— R., 30.
Musgrave, G., 31, 49, 50, 51, 58.
Muttlebury, T., 51.

Nettlecombe, 31.
Nevill, Sir E., 30.
Newcombe, J., 58.
Nicholas, O., 47.
Nicholls, O., 49.

Otterton, 53.
Ottery St. Mary, 60.
Oxford, All Souls, 60.

P. P. (Pretended Prince), 66.

INDEX

Palmer, Major, 57.
—— N., 29, 58.
Pamphlets suppressed, 27.
Parfitt, J., 41, 42.
Paulet, Lord, 24.
—— F., 28, 50.
Pee coats, 56.
Phelips, Sir E., 11, 29, 34, 35, 36, 37, 42, 43, 48, 49.
Piggot, J., 29, 58.
Pitman, S., 27.
Player, W., 30.
Plummer, W., 36, 42, 43.
Polden Hills, 44.
Poole, T., 58.
Porlock, 53.
Portman, J., 58.
—— Sir W., 29, 49, 57, 64.
Postmasters, irregularity, 54.
Prideaux, Mr., 53.
—— E., 4, 6.
Prowse, J., 29.
Pryse, J., 58.
Pyne, Madam, 53.

Questions (The Three), 28.
Quo Warranto issued, 47, 48, 54.

Reading, 64.
Reeves, R., 26.
Reynon, P., 29, 50, 51.
Rodland, W., 32.
Rogers, J., 26.
Rolls, H., 51.
—— Sir J., 52.
Rome, church of, described, 3.

Roynon, H., 58.
—— W., 58.

Salisbury, 56, 62, 64.
Sambourne, T., 58.
Sandford, Mr., 49.
Sandys, J., 58.
Sanford, J., 30, 58.
Sarsfield, Col., 62.
Savage, Mr., 53.
Sedgemoor, 45.
Serge makers, 21.
Seymour, Mr. Speaker, 35, 41.
—— Sir E., 57.
—— T., 57.
Shepton Mallet, 22, 31, 44, 45.
Sherborne, 60, 61, 62, 64.
Smith, Sir J., 29, 52, 58.
Somerset, County, 9, 18, 31, 49, 56, 65, 69, 70.
Southampton, Duke of, 35.
Speak, Mr., 53, 57.
—— Capt., 53.
—— G., 31, 33, 46, 47.
—— J., 31, 32, 33, 48, 49, 50, 51.
Speke, Sir H., 61, 62, 64.
Stawell, Lord, 16, 58.
—— Mr., 57.
Steer, Mr., 16.
Steynings, C., 31, 50.
Stocker, A., 36, 42.
Stonehenge, 64.
Street, 44.
Strode, E., 31, 33, 36, 38, 39, 40, 41, 42, 44, 45, 48, 50, 51, 52.
—— T., 51.

Strode, Col. W., 44.
—— W., 31, 32, 46, 48, 49, 50, 51.
—— W. (bailiff), 37, 42, 43.
—— W. (Shepton), 45.
—— W. (son of Col. W.), 44, 45.
—— W. (Devon), 44.
—— W. (Kent), 45.
Sunderland, Earl of, 27, 44.
Swanswick, 30.
Sydenham, Sir J., 33, 46, 47.
Syderfin, R., 31, 32, 48, 50, 51.
Symes, W., 30.
Symons, W., 26.

Taunton, 4, 6, 11, 17, 21, 32, 47, 49, 53, 65.
Test Act, 2, 15.
Three Questions (The), 28.
Trenchard, J., 4, 6, 32, 47, 49.
Trim, D., 35, 36, 37, 38, 39, 41, 42, 43.
Tucker, J., 35.
Turner, T., 27.
Twiford, Mr., 36.
Twyford, Capt., 42.
Tynte, Sir Halswell, 3, 29, 47, 49.
—— Sir Hugh, 30, 50, 51.

Vaughan, F., 51.

Wade, N., 45.
Walgrave, Lord, 34, 41, 43.

Walrond, H., 29, 50, 51, 58.
Warre, Sir F., 29, 47, 49, 57.
Watts, J., 58.
Webb, Cornet, 63.
—— J., 51, 58.
Wells, 30, 31, 39, 47, 54, 67.

Welstead, H., 58.
Westley, W., 58.
Wickham, G., 58.
—— W., 58.
William, of Orange, 15, 55, 59.
Williams, D., 58.
Willie, T., 58.
Wincanton, 22, 60, 62, 64.

Witham Friary, 22.
Wool, export of, 69.
Wyndham, E., 30, 41.
—— Sir E., 29.
—— Sir T., 30.
—— Col. T., 42, 57.
—— T., 29, 34, 35, 36.

Yeovil, 54, 65.

www.ingramcontent.com/pod-product-compliance
Lightning Source LLC
Chambersburg PA
CBHW031607110426
42742CB00037B/1318